Alan
Roderick.
February
1990

Johnny!

By The Same Author

The Folklore of Gwent
Village Publishing, Cwmbran, 1983 (Second Edition 1986)

The Folklore of Glamorgan
Village Publishing, Cwmbran, 1986.

Unknown Gwent
Village Publishing, Cwmbran, 1986.

The Ghosts of Gwent
Village Publishing, Cwmbran, 1987.

The Music of Fair Tongues
The Story of the Welsh Language in Gwent
Newport National Eisteddfod Committee 1987.

A Gwent Anthology
Christopher Davies (Publishers) Ltd., Swansea, 1988.

Johnny!

The Story of The Happy Warrior

by

Alan Roderick

Heron Press
1990

ISBN 0 9515213 0 6

Printed in Great Britain by The Starling Press
Alexandra Buildings, Risca,
Newport, Gwent

Published by Heron Press
84 Llanthewy Road, Newport, Gwent
NP9 4LA, WALES/CYMRU

INTRODUCTION

A classical straight left has always been one of the most prized possessions in British boxing. When, as in the case of John Michael Basham, this same straight left was allied to tremendous speed around the ring, glorious footwork and a first class boxing brain, well, then it became virtually unbeatable.

It was the straight left which enabled Johnny to rise to the top of his chosen profession, wrest the British title from the grasp of Johnny Summers and reign supreme as "King" of the British welterweights from 1914 to 1920. And what a left. It had both the fans and the men who made their living writing about boxing falling over themselves to sing its praises.

For some it flashed out with the "speed of an adder's tongue." For others it was a rhythmic instrument shooting out "with the accuracy and speed of the piston of a high speed engine." It was a "rapier" landing with "unfailing accuracy" and tantalising the man in the opposite corner. Johnny himself once described it as his "hurting, jarring, scoring left hand."

The owner of this finely-tuned weapon was born in Newport as one of the humblest of Queen Victoria's subjects, but before life had finished with him, he would spar with that same monarch's grandson, taste triumph and disaster and rub shoulders with some of the richest and most influential men of his day. He would survive two World Wars, live under five different monarchs and take all the hard knocks that boxing and life would throw at him.

The Newport Johnny grew up in, the Newport of the 1890s, was a far cry from the sleepy fishing village of almost a century before. In 1801, the "town's" population was barely a thousand souls — most of them Welsh speaking — but by the time Johnny grew up it had changed out of all recognition. Gone were the Welsh speaking fishermen who had filled the inns and taverns of the town with their songs and plaintive harp music.

In their place were English speaking immigrants from all parts of Britain and Ireland attracted by the lush "pickings" to be made from the flourishing iron and coal industries. Johnny himself came of immigrant stock. His father was an Englishman and his mother's people were Irish. There was, therefore, in the beginning, almost nothing Welsh about Johnny save his birthplace. Yet, in time, he was to become one of the most truly Welsh of all champions, the "darling of Wales" as he was known.

At the time of Johnny's birth, sport was already well established in Newport but it was the oval ball which chiefly occupied the minds of the town's sportsmen. Newport Athletic Club had been founded fifteen years before in 1875 and had already enjoyed four invincible seasons. The club had produced its fair share of heroes and rugby players like Arthur Gould and Jim Hannan were household names, but they were not the kind of men that fired the imagination of the young Johnny Basham. Perhaps inevitably, with a name like his, Johnny's mind was set on boxing.

It was a good time to take up the sport. The days of the bare knuckle fist fighter were over and the Victorian ideal of "manly" and "scientific" boxing was becoming more widespread. From 1900 onwards, in countless halls up and down the country, men were putting on the gloves to box each other for money.

Technically speaking, Johnny was only just a "Victorian," being barely eleven years old when the great queen died, but Victorian or not, in the boxing ring he soon made himself the idol of all Wales and of a good few Englishmen besides. With a name like Basham he might have been expected to be a mere slugger, a "cart-horse" intent only on battering his man to defeat in the quickest possible manner, but Johnny was an artist, a true will-o-the-wisp of the roped square.

Inside the ring he was all "light and fire" as he danced an intricate pattern around his opponent. Tapping out an elegant message with that wonderful left, he graced his chosen profession with a skill that few other boxers have come close to matching.

It was boxing that made Johnny a "star." It put him on a par with the likes of Jim Driscoll, Jimmy Wilde and Freddy Welsh, Wales's three other classic boxers. In a world where television was unknown, radio was barely in its infancy and the newspapers provided most people with their sources of information, such men were celebrities in their own right, the "pop stars" of their day.

Unlike Driscoll, Wilde and Welsh, however, Johnny never went to America and he never fought for a world title, (the Great War probably interfered with that ambition) but there is a sense in which he was more profoundly "Welsh" than any of the others. They drew their support from a relatively narrow base. Driscoll was closely identified with Cardiff, Welsh with Pontypridd and Wilde with the Rhondda. Johnny cast his net wider.

Although born in Newport, he was often classed as an honorary North Walian — he did, after all, live in Wrexham for many years and trained for all of his big fights there. His stay in Wrexham brought him the love and affection of thousands of North Walians and in this way, he united the fans of both North and South Wales in his own person, having fought not only in Wrexham but also in Swansea, Cardiff and Newport. He also enjoyed a devoted following amongst the fight fans of Liverpool and the North of England.

Boxing was good to Johnny. It was his escape from the humdrum existence of the dead-end job and it took him out of the narrow confines of his small-town background, opening up fresh horizons. Indeed, it is probably no exaggeration to say that boxing may well have saved his life during the terrible carnage of the First World War. As the champion and Lonsdale-belt holder, Johnny was in something of a privileged position and far too valuable to the military authorities to risk losing in the lottery that was the fate of the frontline troops. Others were not so lucky. Two of Johnny's contemporaries, Tom McCormick and Dai Roberts, both of whom he fought and beat, met their deaths in action in France. Many another boxer failed to survive the war.

Boxing also provided Johnny with wealth, fame and glamour. At his peak he was earning thousands of pounds. Yet, for all the benefits it brought, boxing was a hard taskmaster. Eleven times Johnny went the full distance of twenty-three-minute-rounds and the relentlessly gruelling battles he fought with that implacable opponent, Ted "Kid" Lewis, the one man Johnny could never beat, took their mental and physical toll.

Boxing also brought tragedy in its wake — although he could not be blamed, Johnny was, ultimately, "responsible" for the untimely death of a fellow boxer, the memory of which stayed with him for the rest of his life and must have left some scars. And when the boxing was over, another struggle began. But this time the struggle was against destitution, poverty and the slow slide into obscurity from all of which Johnny had originally made his escape through boxing.

He had only himself to blame, of course. He made money but it went through his fingers like the waters of his native river Usk. Even when he was earning thousands, he spent it. When he was not spending it himself, he gave it away to friends and the hangers-on that invariably gather around a successful fighter. In this respect he was no different to Jim Driscoll and Freddy Welsh, both of whom won and lost a fortune. Like them, Johnny was generous to a fault. He turned out innumerable times for charity at Assaults-at-arms and exhibition bouts even turning out as a forward in a charity football match.

Johnny's was the classic rags to riches and straight-back-down-again story. After his three terrific tussles with Ted "Kid" Lewis, his fistic powers deserted him and he became a sad shadow of his former self. He tried his hand at various jobs and then, when nothing seemed to stick, he wandered the country looking for work and a place to stay.

And when the money had gone, there was always the drink. By the end of his life, it has to be said, Johnny liked his drop of drink. Cliff Curvis, the Swansea boxer, and himself a British Welterweight champion, remembers a BBC Radio programme he did with Johnny just before he died. Forty years later, he can still recall the producers of the day sending out for beer to keep Johnny on the premises. Had they allowed Johnny to quench his thirst in a nearby pub, the likelihood was that they would never have got him back again...

Yet despite it all, despite the poverty, the poor health, and the dependence on drink, Johnny still had a smile on his lips. Not for nothing was he known as "Laughing Johnny Basham," "The Happy Warrior." All the bouquets, all the slings and arrows life could find to throw at him, he accepted with the same resolute good humour. Through it all — through the good times and the bad — when the hard-earned money was gone and the bright lights and cheering crowds were no more, Johnny could still enjoy a laugh and a joke. But then that was Johnny Basham all over — The Happy Warrior was just built that way.

LIST OF CONTENTS

CHAPTER I

Birth Of A Boxer

"I Was Tempted To Try My Hand At The Boxing Game And Strolled Into A Boxing Booth. I Walked Out With Two Black Eyes."

Johnny Basham's first boxing gloves were school caps wrapped round his fists, his first opponents boys of his own age from St. Mary's Primary School, Newport. With a name like Basham he was almost bound to fight and it did not take him long to defeat the competition and make himself the school's uncrowned champion. It was to be the start of a long and brilliant career. A career which would take him from the poverty of his early childhood to undreamt of riches.

Johnny was born John Michael Basham (John for his mother's brother, Michael for her father) on September 13th, 1889 and baptised on October 6th of that year. This is the date given in the Baptismal register of St. Mary's Church, Newport, but for some reason, most boxing records give the year of his birth as 1890.

Johnny's mother, Ellen Basham, had married Edward Basham, a mason's labourer, at the Registry Office in Newport on July 23rd, 1883. She was the daughter of Irish born Michael Mahoney, a factory labourer, but had herself been born in Newport. Unusually for the close of the nineteenth century, all four of the witnesses present at Ellen and Edward's wedding could read and write.

Edward Basham was the son of William Basham, a labourer born in Cambridge and Ann Basham from Ireland. Edward himself had been born in Brompton, Kent. As Ellen's mother, Anne, had also been born in Ireland, it is perhaps not too far fetched to imagine that most of the blood running in Johnny's veins was the "fighting blood" of the Irish with just a little tincture of English "to top up the mixture."

Certainly Johnny was well set up to be a fighter: he had his incomparable name, his Irish blood — and it is remarkable how many boxing champions the Irish have produced — and also, having been born in Newport, he was Welsh by birth. As an old boxing booth fighter once remarked to the novelist Alexander Cordell, author of "The Rape of The Fair Country," "We're Welshmen, we've got to fight." Last but certainly not least, as the great Jack Dempsey used to say : "A good fighter is a hungry fighter."

Johnny Basham may not have been starving to death, but he was not living in the lap of luxury either. Ellen Basham is said to have had seventeen children — whatever the truth of this, she certainly brought ten children into the world of whom only eight survived, five girls and three boys — and before her marriage at the age of nineteen, she had been a servant in a nut and bolt factory. Her husband, Edward, was the son of a platelayer so that money was not in plentiful supply in the Basham household.

Life was hard for the Bashams as it was for the vast majority of their fellow townsmen, and the young Johnny Basham soon learnt that he was required to make a contribution to the family budget. He cast around for a source of income and found the answer when a friend suggested he should sell newspapers. Soon he was out on the streets, bare-footed, selling his bundle of papers to anyone who would buy. The newspaper game supplemented his income and that of his family, but it often brought Johnny into conflict with his religious duties:

"Wild as I was, and I WAS wild, I had been taught by my parents to be a good Catholic, and it hurt like Old Nick to have to miss my duties on a Sunday morning in order to sell papers; but what could I do? Bread was wanted, and I was a bread-winner, so out I went with my papers, and missed my church.

"And here is the sequel. Every Monday morning the teacher used to start off with the same question: Hands up all those who were not at Church yesterday, and every Monday morning it was Johnny Basham's hand that shot up first, and out I would walk to receive the regular dose of two slaps 'in the same place' for the shocking neglect of my religious duties.

"I suppose that, had I explained the reason of my absence, and how badly my few coppers were needed, I would have been forgiven, but I somehow could not face explaining before all the class, so I continued to 'take my medicine'."

From newspapers, Johnny progressed to "spare boy" at the Newport Glass and Bottle Works where his work consisted of carrying beer for the bottle makers. For this he earned seven shillings (35 pence) a week plus the few pence the men chose to give him. Before long his wages increased to ten shillings (fifty pence) a week plus bonus, but Johnny had not forgotten his boxing:

"During the idle hours when on night shift, we used to pass the time

away having friendly bouts with a set of old boxing gloves, and somehow or another I took to the boxing game like a duck takes to water, and soon could do as I liked with my pals at the bottle works.

"This began to be talked about, and at last I was persuaded to enter a boys' competition in the boxing booth of that well-known showman, Jack Scarrott, who has had, I should think, every champion of Wales in his booth at one time or another.

"I won't make a long story about that competition. Let me just say that I won it and received for work done the princely sum of fifteen shillings, and a pat on the back from Mr. Scarrott, who told me to stick at the game and I would make a good 'un.

"I have earned big money since those days with the aid of my fists, but even the biggest purse I ever pulled down never gave me the thrill that I felt when I felt those fifteen shillings chinking in my hands!"

Those lines were written by Johnny for the "Empire News" in 1929. Yet in an interview he gave in 1913, he recalled that his first experience of the ring was at a fair in Newport. *"I was tempted to try my hand at the boxing game,"* he said *"and strolled into a boxing booth. I walked out with two black eyes."*

A case of memory playing tricks perhaps? However that may be, it was certainly Johnny's love of boxing which caused him to lose his job at the bottle works. He had been matched against another young hopeful, called Murphy, from the Pill area of Newport, and they met at the Royal Field Artillery Barracks overlooking the town. Down went Johnny, knocked out in the second round and, the very next day, he was out for the count again, this time dismissed from his job at the bottle works for taking time off without permission.

Even this did not dampen his enthusiasm for boxing and he began to try his luck against the other young men in the town. At that time there were various clubs and halls scattered throughout Newport where boxing contests could be staged and Johnny found himself fighting young men of his own age like E. Thomas, T. Scrivens and Boxer Ryan, the last two both coming from Pill.

At this stage Johnny was fighting chiefly for medals and trophies but already his great talent was beginning to be recognised. In one early fight against F. Sydney at the Tredegar Hall on Wednesday, July 7th, 1909, the local reporter was impressed by Johnny's "grand reach" and cleverness and recognised that he was "endowed with a very big heart." He predicted a great future for Johnny in the fight game, provided he could get a backer with financial muscle behind him.

An early portrait of a serious looking Johnny (seated on the right of the picture)

And there, in the proverbial nutshell, was Johnny's problem. In those early days, few people wanted to know about boxers from Newport, the accepted wisdom was that it was useless to look outside Cardiff and the Rhondda for boxers of any merit. And in any case, to the casual observer, Johnny scarcely looked like a boxer. He was tall and slim, lanky with long arms and legs and his chest and shoulders needed expansion. He also suffered from nerves, but he got over this after his first few big contests. His training was done at the Crindau Working Men's Club, his sparring partners being local lads like himself.

People began to sit up and take notice though after his fight with Boxer Ryan. The aptly named "Boxer" was a Pill boy and he wanted to show that he, and not Basham, was the man to beat in Newport. They met in an Assault-at-arms at the Campbell Bannerman Hall in Newport's Wharf road on Monday, October 18th, 1909. A £20 trophy was at stake, plus of course the reputations of both men.

"Young Basham of Crindau," as he was now being billed, and the "Boxer" touched gloves and the fight was underway. Both men looked extremely fit and both had brought their supporters with them — there is, of course, no rivalry like a local rivalry. Johnny's reach was longer but Ryan was altogether sturdier and firmer set. From the beginning it was the Pill boy who forced the pace and he drove Basham to the ropes, but Johnny fought back with coolness and considerable determination. Time and again, his fine footwork got him out of dangerous situations.

In the second round, Boxer Ryan made it clear that he wanted to end the fight as quickly as possible. He drove Johnny to the ropes continually but the Crindau youth seemed content to soak up the punishment and allow Ryan to dictate the fight. Then, suddenly, Johnny took over. He stopped Ryan's forward march with a straight left and a right swing to the region of the heart and round two finished with honours fairly even. Then, in the third, Johnny quickly began to pile up the points and soon it was Ryan's turn to have his back to the ropes. A Basham left passed over his shoulder and then a nasty right hook sent the "Boxer" to the floor. At this point the Basham supporters went wild with delight and made so much noise that the timekeeper's count could not be heard.

After the fight, Boxer Ryan's seconds insisted that their man had only been down for eight seconds and had not been counted out, but the referee would have none of it. He, at least, was in no doubt that Basham was the winner on a knock out and awarded the fight to him, a decision which met with almost universal approval. With Boxer Ryan out of the way, there was no one left to fight in Newport, and Johnny began to look further afield for potential opponents. Luckily, he now had a backer, Captain Evans of Chepstow, the adjutant of the Monmouthshire volunteers. A number of Evans's brother officers had also decided to back Johnny.

Accordingly, arrangements were made for Johnny to fight Fred Dyer of Cardiff. At the end of December, 1909 the two men signed articles to box each other for ten three-minute rounds at the Newport Drill Hall on New Year's Day, 1910, a Saturday. The fight was for £25 a-side and a £20 purse, the winner to take £15, the loser £5. The fight was to be part of an Assault-at-arms held to assist the funds of the First Monmouthshire Regiment. The purse was provided by Captain Evans and the referee was G.T. Dunning of the "Sportsman."

Fred Dyer was known as the "singing boxer." He had a "good, well-trained and naturally sweet voice, of no little power and compass" and he was not afraid to use it. He was also an all-round athlete with trophies for walking, running, swimming, boxing and singing. His best performance in the ring had come during his two fights as an amateur and, in the Amateur Championship, when he had won his first heat and lost the second on points.

Fred trained quietly for the match with his brother in Cardiff whilst Johnny prepared under the supervision of Boyo Driscoll. On the morning of the fight, the weigh-in at the "Evening Express" office was attended by a number of local sportsmen, including Johnny's backer, Captain Evans. Both Basham and Dyer were well under the weight. Dyer, attended by his brother Joe, scaled nine stone nine pounds, whilst Johnny, attended by Boyo Driscoll, weighed in at nine stone seven pounds.

A big crowd gathered at the Drill Hall on that New Year's Day, 1910 for what amounted to Johnny's professional debut. Fred welcomed him by banging Johnny flush on the nose but Johnny's answer nearly finished the fight there and then, his crashing blow to the solar plexus almost dropping Dyer to the canvas, as the Cardiff man later admitted.

In round two, the "singing boxer" started to regain his confidence, but he overreached himself on one occasion and fell. Now Johnny showed his inexperience. Instead of staying calm and biding his time, he threw caution to the winds and punched out wildly. Dyer was able to protect himself and then launch a series of counter attacks.

The third round was all Dyer and Johnny just could not keep Fred's straight left away from his nose, although he shook him once with a blow to the head. In reply, Dyer rapped out three more lefts, once again the target being Johnny's nose. The crowd roared their approval as the Newport man rushed in, but again Dyer covered up well.

When the bell went for round four, Johnny made what proved to be his last stand, firing off lefts and rights at a frenetic pace. But Dyer was not to be denied. He dug one into Johnny's ribs and then pounded away to his face. Johnny fell onto the ropes and, when he bounced back, the "singing boxer" was waiting. "Crack" went Dyer's hand on Johnny's jaw. Down went Johnny for the count. Everywhere there was pandemonium and terrific excitement. Amidst all the noise and din, it was Fred Dyer who helped to carry Johnny's limp frame back to his corner. The noise was so tremendous that no one had heard the gong and the referee had to ask for silence. When order was eventually restored, the referee was able to tell the crowd that Johnny had been saved by the bell and he had not been counted out. But it made no difference to the actual result as Johnny refused to carry on, claiming his thumbs had been knocked out, and it was Fred Dyer's hand that the referee raised in victory.

It was, it must be said, hardly a triumph for the Newport boxer. He had been defeated and defeated badly. Many of those who left the Stow Hill Drill Hall that night after watching Johnny's inglorious debut could have been forgiven for thinking that he had better go back to the glass works. They must have consigned him to the deepest depths of the pugilistic scrap heap, and who could blame them? They were not to know that they had just seen a future champion in the making and that that champion would not be famed for the quality of his singing voice.

Johnny's long climb from obscurity had begun but, at the first attempt, he had suffered a set back. That climb seemed never ending when, in his second professional outing, he once more plunged to defeat. Again it was a Cardiff man who did the damage. Badger Brian was sparring partner to the great Jim Driscoll and had been around the master long enough to learn a few of his tricks.

At the Badminton Club in Cardiff on January 29th, 1910 Johnny wisely insisted on clean breaks right from the start of the fifteen round contest and relied on his height and long reach to keep the dangerous Brian at bay. The tactics worked a treat until the fourth round when, in front of the packed club, Badger landed a vicious right hook and Johnny failed to get up. The referee, Danny Davies of Merthyr, counted him out.

For the next few months, Johnny enjoyed mixed fortunes. He restored some much needed self confidence by beating Billy McKeiver in three rounds at Chepstow but promptly went back to his bad old ways when he allowed Harry Lawrence to k.o. him in the first round. A draw and two successive one-round victories went some way to wiping out the memory of that particular defeat but even then Johnny's record was scarcely that of a world beater.

He needed a boost quickly and he got it — not by any feats of fistic brilliance in the ring — but through the drastic decision of joining the army. At the beginning of 1911 he enlisted in the Royal Welch Fusiliers. It was one of those decisions which change a man's life forever. It certainly changed Johnny Basham's life.

Eventually, that decision would see him transformed from little more than a boxing no-hoper into the "Happy Warrior," one of the cleverest and most scientific boxers that British fight fans had ever seen. Johnny had always shown talent: now that talent was to be honed and sharpened and polished into something very near fistic genius.

CHAPTER II

The Fighting Fusilier

"We Had Hot, Spluttering Paraffin Lamps, Which Every Now And Then Spilled A Drop Of Almost Boiling Paraffin Oil Onto The Neck Of Whichever Boxer Happened To Be Below."

The Regiment that Johnny had joined had a long and honourable tradition stretching back to the time of James II and William of Orange. Its soldiers had fought for King and Country in the War of the Spanish Succession, the Seven Years War and the Napoleonic Wars. They had seen action in the Crimean War, the Ashanti Wars and the Burma Campaign of 1855. They were there helping to fight the Boers and to put down the Boxer rebellion in China. They would soon be manning trenches along the Somme and at Ypres, but that was still in the future. Since 1877, their headquarters had been at Wrexham.

In many ways, Wrexham was the most "English" town in North Wales. The language of its people was English, though there was a large Welsh speaking minority. For at least the next fifteen years, it would be Johnny Basham's home, he would marry there and it was there that he would do all of his training for his most important fights. The people of Wrexham would take him to their hearts and treat him as one of their own. Significantly, for his future career, Wrexham was within striking distance of the prestigious Liverpool Stadium, the premier boxing venue in the north of England.

At the beginning, though, Wrexham meant a change of name. Henceforth, it would not be "Young Basham" appearing in the ring, but "Private Basham." Later, it would be "Corporal Basham" and, finally, "Sergeant Basham." Regarding his name, Johnny was fond of telling a story about his early days at Wrexham Barracks, days when "Basham" was still far from being a household name. Eyeing the new recruit, a sergeant would bark out the question, "Name?" "Basham, Johnny, sir" came the quick reply. Suspecting his leg was being pulled, the sergeant turned to Johnny's companion. "Name?" he barked again. "Champion, George, sir," came the equally prompt reply. Now the sergeant was convinced his leg was being pulled. "Right, you two," he bawled. "I've got a job for you — you can clean out the guard room."

Some time later, the same sergeant happened to spy Johnny and his friend again. He asked the same questions and got exactly the same answers, whereupon he bellowed at the two young soldiers in a voice of thunder: "Right, you two, then scrub the tables in the mess till I can see my face in them, perhaps then, you'll stop trying to be smart with me!"

But it did not take long for the Royal Welch Fusiliers to discover Johnny's talent for boxing. The officers of the RWF regarded boxing as a scientific and healthy sport guaranteed to bring out the best in the men under their command. Soon Johnny was featuring in contests at the Wrexham Barracks Gymnasium and in fights at the Wrexham Drill Hall, organised by the Liverpool Stadium management. Amongst those he took on and beat at Wrexham were Dick Knock of Leicester, Harry Jones of Cardiff and Harry Berry of Dublin, the featherweight champion of Ireland. Major Gabeth, Commander of the Wrexham Depot, willingly gave his permission for Basham to take part in these contests. They were invariably well attended and Johnny inevitably impressed the crowds with his cleverness and his "clean, manly and scientific boxing."

Occasionally, the opponent was a fellow soldier, as in this bout which took place on Wednesday, October 29th, 1913 at the Wrexham Barracks Gymnasium:

"The tit-bit of the evening was provided in a ten three-minute round contest by Private Johnny Basham, who is recognised as one of the finest exponents of the day, and Lance Sergeant Spalding of Portland, the middleweight finalist of the Irish Army in 1912, the winner of the Southern Command middleweight of 1913, and finalist of the All Army and Navy Championship Meeting, 1913.

"Spalding was the heavier man by sixteen pounds, and there was a good deal of speculation as to how Basham would fare against his powerfully built antagonist. It was evident from the start that Spalding was a fighter and hankered for close quarters, but Basham gave nothing away, and contented himself with left leads to the head, side stepping, and with jumping to administer severe body blows and hugging to avoid punishment. He gave a wonderful exhibition of ringcraft and was too slippery for the muscular Southerner, who was quite unable to indulge in in-fighting, a method which would naturally have suited him much better.

"He was a keen and dogged opponent, however, and occasionally gave Basham a reminder that it was unwise to take liberties with him. Basham, however, gained points in every round, and in the eighth

delivered a powerful body blow which resulted in his opponent being counted out. As a solid standup fighter, Spalding — who, by the way, was several times cautioned for hitting low — gave one the impression of a difficult man to beat, but against Basham's craft and scientific methods he was outclassed."

Occasionally, however, and especially at the start of his career with the RWF, Johnny would venture outside the confines of the barracks and into the colourful world of the boxing booth. He had already experienced the booths as a boy in Newport, but Harry Hughes's booth was something different:

"I got a glorious chance when Wrexham March Fair came around, for with the fair came Harry Hughes with one of the best known and best conducted boxing booths that travelled England. No ordinary boxing show was the big, well set-up affair with which this ex-dragoon toured the fairgrounds of Britain.

"I shall never forget what a great sight it was to see those two horsemen in full dragoon kit (I understand by special permission of the Government). One each side of the booth door they stood, each on a huge black horse whose coat shone like polished ebony. These men used to go through all the lance exercises in the small confines of the boxing booth, and I have heard many a gasp as the lance has passed, seemingly by chance, within a hairbreadth of some bystander! It was no ordinary show that booth of Harry Hughes!"

Egged on by his soldier comrades, Johnny was persuaded to chance his arm against the son of the booth owner, Billy Hughes, who had recently defeated Young Josephs over fifteen rounds, at Hull. As Johnny pulled on the gloves, the booth seemed to be filled with members of the Royal Welch Fusiliers and he began to wonder how on earth he was going to box, as the roped off square set aside for the boxing was completely filled with spectators. He need not have worried. Hughes senior roared at the crowd, telling them to:

"Pull the ropes well back, give the lads who are boxing breathing room, and, please, no remarks, do all you have to do with the clap of the hand!"

And with that they were off. It was fast and furious stuff and Johnny had his work cut out against the tricky Billy Hughes but he did enough to impress Billy's father who asked him how he would like to fight Charlie Milestone, of Chester.

Milestone was known to be a tough customer with a good, solid punch and, in some quarters, he was claimed to be the lightweight champion of the North. At first Johnny hesitated, but then agreed, provided he could get the necessary permission from his commanding officer. This proved to be easier than anticipated, the C.O raising no objections as long as Johnny remembered he was a Royal Welch Fusilier first and foremost and that the honour of the regiment was paramount.

Expecting a bigger crowd than usual, the shrewd Harry Hughes had cleverly added a couple of shutters to the side of his booth, thus increasing its capacity by at least a third, and even then the spectators were rapidly finding out what it felt like to be a sardine in a tin when Johnny made his appearance.

There being no changing rooms, he had to shelter behind the greatcoats of two friends and prepare himself as best he could. Then the referee, Mr. Bert Hughes, called the two boxers to him: *"Now then, you fellows, we want NO fancy stuff, we want a FIGHT; no fight, no money, SO GO TO IT."*

The fight was scheduled for ten rounds and the "arena" could not have presented a greater contrast to the Pudsey street Stadium in Liverpool or the Covent Garden headquarters of the National Sporting Club:

"Packed denser, by far, than the cheapest seats at a cup-tie were the crowd, the ring ropes were held back by those nearest to them, and went taut or slack, according to the excitement of the holders.

"In place of the white blazing lamps overhead seen in the big halls, we had hot, spluttering paraffin lamps, which every now and then spilled a drop of almost boiling paraffin oil onto the neck of whichever boxer happened to be below. I will say this for those lamps; they played no favourites; Milestone got just as much as I did."

Johnny defeated Milestone on points and, for his night's work, was paid the sum of thirty shillings (£1-50) plus five shillings (25p) extra from Harry Hughes. The money soon disappeared into the pockets of Mr. Pofords Esq., fish and chip proprietor Wrexham, as Johnny and his military mates indulged in a veritable orgy of fish, chips and lemonade, washed down by gallons of tea from the Army canteen on their return to Barracks.

As Johnny's fame grew, so did his following. For fights outside Wrexham, he was accompanied by a dedicated band of soldiers, any one of whom could expect to fall foul of Johnny's wicked sense of fun if they were not totally on their guard. Johnny's C.O. had warned him more than once about his clowning and love of jokes. "See here, Basham," he said. "Believe you me, those sky-larking tricks of yours will get you into serious trouble one day if you're not very careful." Luckily for Johnny, his C.O. was not around on the night he pulled the trick with the railway tickets . . .

"One night after a fight we were as usual making merry in the refreshment room of the station, and in the good natured horse-play that was

Johnny with two soldier comrades

going on one of the boys dropped his return half of his railway ticket and never noticed it.

"Some imp of mischief entered my head, and I picked up the ticket, unseen by anyone and, never saying a word, I put it in my pocket to await developments. The usual last-second rush to the train, the usual commandeering of a carriage so that we could play penny "nap," and we settled down like hardened gamblers to while away the time on the long journey.

"At last came what I had been waiting for, the brakes began to grind and the train started to pull up at the station, where tickets were collected. 'Tickets, boys,' I said, and with that I produced my own, and being nearest the door held my hand out for the others, so that as soon as the collector opened the door he could be handed the tickets and get on with his business.

"All the boys except the one whose ticket I had picked up tossed their bits of cardboard to me, but he, poor beggar, was searching all his pockets as if he had lost a hundred pound note. At last he gasped: "I have lost my brief, what shall I do?"

"Oh, get under the seat," said I. "This joker will only bob in and bob out again; you will be as safe as houses." So under the seat he scrambled, in the dust, to wait till the collector had been and gone; but this was where I came in!

"Winking at the rest of the boys, I showed them that I had his ticket, but by signs let them know that they must not breathe a word.

"At last the door opened, and in came the collector. By pretending to fiddle about I got him suspicious, so suspicious that when I did give him the tickets he counted them over twice, and then counted the occupants of the carriage. "What's this?" he said. "There are eight tickets, and there are only seven of you in the carriage?"

"Oh, that's all right, sir," I said: "our friend is under the seat; he likes travelling that way best. Don't you, Bob?"

"And with that I moved away and revealed the dusty, startled face of our chum!

"The collector walked away, muttering about damn fools, but, oh! if he could have heard the flow of language that dusty Welch Fusilier turned out when he had managed to come up for air, he would have hidden his head in shame to think what a novice he was at the cussin' game!

"However, the boy took it in good part, and we were all as happy as sandboys when we arrived at our destination."

It was this same sense of fun which earned Johnny a part in the Wrexham pantomime one year. On Saturday, February 21st, 1914 the

"Wrexham Advertiser" noted in its pages that, as a special attraction, the cast of "Babes In The Wood" had prevailed upon Widow Winkle to challenge "Champion Basham" to a two-round contest to be fought to the bitter end, excepting a knockout blow. Private Basham had willingly accepted the challenge and the Widow Winkle would be seconded by Sam Soapsuds.

But not everyone in North Wales loved a boxer, not even one as successful as Johnny. The Rhos Free Church, for example, made strenuous efforts to stop a boxing exhibition involving Johnny going ahead at the Rhos Pavilion in July, 1914. A deputation from the Free Church Council waited upon the management and later held an interview with Johnny, but liabilities had been incurred by all the parties concerned and the boxing went ahead, against the wishes of the church. Eventually, the exhibition started and there was no sign of opposition either inside or outside the pavilion. The large crowd gave Johnny a great ovation and he entertained them, together with his exhibition partners, Young Pierce, of Oswestry and Fred Rowland from Wrexham. Johnny amazed the crowd with his "wonderful agility" and he was loudly cheered at the end.

Many tales are told of Johnny's time with the Royal Welch Fusiliers. One story current in its day concerned the veteran bare-fist fighter from South Wales, who was a model of decorum and an excellent soldier when sober, but once he had got a few pints inside him... His party piece was to return to camp after a Saturday night out on the beer and loudly proclaim his contempt for "glove boxers" in general and Johnny Basham in particular. Having got that off his chest, he would then loudly and repeatedly challenge Johnny to a fight.

Of course, it was more than Johnny's reputation was worth to be mixed up in a drunken brawl with an ageing bare-knuckle fighter so he was always told well in advance when Mr. Thomas, for such was the mountain fighter's name, would be likely to make an appearance. Johnny then took good care to make himself scarce. This had no effect on Thomas who continued to shout at anyone who would listen that Johnny Basham was nothing but a lily-livered coward for refusing to fight with him.

The odd thing was that during the rest of the week, when Thomas was sober, he never bothered, insulted or challenged Johnny in any way. His regular Saturday night shenanigans, however, were a source of rich weekend entertainment as far as his fellow Royal Welch Fusiliers were concerned.

CHAPTER III
Liverpool's Own

"Get On With Your Boxing,
Growled Referee Smith."

Johnny Basham had started his professional boxing career by boxing in small halls, clubs, boxing booths and the Wrexham Barracks Gymnasium but he had never boxed at a venue of any great size. All that changed when he was asked to box at the famous Liverpool Stadium. The Pudsey street arena was capable of holding up to 5,000 spectators and was one of the premier boxing venues in the north of England. When a fighter was asked to box there, he knew he was "getting somewhere."

Johnny's first fight in Liverpool Stadium came about through his RWF connections. One day, he was summoned to the Wrexham Barracks gymnasium for a meeting with Staff-Sergeant Bradley. At first, Johnny feared the worst, but his apprehension turned to joy when the Staff-Sergeant asked him if he would like to fight at the Stadium.

As Master of Ceremonies at the Stadium, Bradley knew all the right people and a good word from him could be just the thing to start a young boxer off on the road to glory. Naturally, Johnny was delighted to accept the offer and, on September 23rd, 1911, he stepped into the ring at the Pudsey street stadium against Frank Baker, then the idol of the Liverpool fans and a claimant to the light-weight championship of the North of England.

It was a dream debut. That night Johnny outpointed his opponent over fifteen rounds much to the delight of his travelling band of supporters:

"I'll bet those Liverpool sportsmen thought that it was some sort of a military tournament when they arrived that night, for there were soldiers everywhere. What lads those Welch fusiliers were. They had obtained leave on every possible excuse — from dying grandmothers to the marriage of a favourite sister."

Johnny was paid five pounds in silver for the Baker fight by the manager of the Stadium, Major Arnold Wilson, and most of that was gone by the time he returned home to Wrexham:

"We boys of the Welch Fusiliers were in high glee as we travelled back

home, and by the time I had again stood treats many times round at Mr. Pofords's saloon, and paid my footing in the canteen, the five pounds had dwindled away like a light fall of snow before a morning's sun."

So Johnny's attitude to money was already well established: if he had it, he spent it. If his friends were there to spend it with him, so much the better. It was an attitude which would continue even when the big purses were coming in, and he was at the height of his fame. It was an attitude which, ultimately, would lead to his downfall and a life of poverty but, in those early days in Liverpool, Johnny had no qualms, no thoughts for the future:

"Why should I worry? Wasn't I healthy? Wasn't I happy in my job? Life was just a big lark and boxing the best fun of all, so what mattered it where or how the few quid went?"

The Frank Baker fight marked the beginning of a long and lasting association between Johnny Basham and the famous Stadium which would see him fight there some forty times over a period of eight years. His record included 32 victories, three draws, three exhibition matches and only four defeats. Small wonder, then, that he was to earn for himself the title of "Liverpool's Own."

The men that Johnny fought during his time at Liverpool read like a "Who's Who" of British and European Boxing in the early years of the twentieth century — there was rugged Gus Platts, the Yorkshireman from Sheffield, Johnny Summers, the man from London's Canning Town, Eddie Beattie and Tom McCormick, both of whom later challenged Johnny for his British Welterweight title.

There were fellow Welshmen Will Brooks and Dai Roberts, Europeans such as the hard-hitting Swiss, Albert Badoud, the Frenchmen Henri Demien and Fernand Quendreux, and the Dane with the English sounding name, "Dick Nelson." Then there were the honest journeymen like Dick Knock, Mick Gordon and George Colebourne, not forgetting the visitors from America — Joe Hurst, Young Ahearn, "The Dancing Master," and Frank Madole.

Ah, Frank Madole. Scarcely a name to conjure with in boxing circles today, but it was a name that Johnny never forgot and one that occupied his thoughts for many a long day. Madole had come to Britain in order to, as he put it, see the country and "collect a little easy money on the way." He had a long string of victories over the best American fighters to his credit and obviously fancied his chances with Johnny Basham.

The Liverpool Stadium was packed as the two fighters received their instructions from referee Frank Bradley, then the editor of the "Mirror of Life," on June 19th, 1913. Bradley wasted no time in preliminaries. He told Basham and Madole: *"You boys don't need telling the game: all I want is a good, clean contest."*

That Madole had other ideas was amply demonstrated in the second round when he appeared to deliberately aim a low punch at Johnny. The punch had the desired effect as it literally turned Johnny sick and he was in pain when he retreated to his corner. But if that was bad enough, there was worse to come:

"The third session was hardly half-way through when my opponent ripped in a wallop that sent me down writhing. Men got up from their seats at the ringside, shook their fists at Madole, and yelled "Foul" to the referee. I am told that they yelled other words beside "foul," but I was suffering too much to hear what anyone said!"

The referee ignored all cries of "foul" and began his count but Johnny was saved by the bell. During the interval Johnny refused to continue with the fight and pulled his protection cup out of his shorts to prove his point. Despite the evidence of the cup which was broken in two the referee insisted that he had "seen no sign of a low blow" and awarded the fight to Madole. It was the American's first fight in Britain and he could not have made a more controversial debut.

Johnny burned for a re-match and he got one — on July 3rd, 1913. If there had been any doubts about the first fight, there were none about the second. Right from the start, Johnny tore into his man and the tactics worked as the referee stopped the fight in the first round, to save Madole from further punishment. Two weeks later, they met again for the third and last time. They managed to go the full fifteen rounds, but Johnny Basham was in no doubt that he was a deserved winner on points:

"Two weeks later we met before a house that was sold out, I think, before the first preliminary fight went into the ring. I won't waste a lot of space talking about this fight. The decision will be the explanation of it all if I use one of the American's own phrases: "What I did at that boy was a shame." No, I didn't knock him out, but I larrupped him that well that I'll bet he says a little prayer every time he hears the name of Wales mentioned!"

Thankfully, such "grudge" fights were the exception rather than the rule at the Liverpool Stadium. Most boxers had their own code of sportsmanlike conduct to which they usually kept. Of course, the contests were hard fought affairs with no quarter given and none asked for, but the fighters rarely lost their innate sense of "chivalry" towards one other. Often, if one man slipped down, his opponent would help him to rise, or stand back until he had got to his feet again. There seems, too, to have been none of the menacing "eyeballing" prevalent in all too many of today's contests. It is hard to imagine Johnny "eyeballing" anyone — with the possible exception of Frank Madole, perhaps. The "Happy Warrior" would have been more likely to collapse into helpless laughter than to fix his man with a lethal stare before their fight began.

The fight with Denmark's Dick Nelson at the Liverpool Stadium on March 12th, 1914, which Johnny won on points over fifteen rounds, proved that a sense of fair play was by no means confined to British born fighters. The "Fighting Dane" was, rather confusingly, referred to as an "American" by the sports correspondents attending the fight. Nelson had beaten Johnny Summers and his rugged style gave Johnny some trouble, but the Welshman's "beautiful footwork" was usually enough to get him out of danger and he eventually triumphed after a "rousing finish" from both boxers.

Business as usual then for Johnny, but what lifts this fight out of the ordinary is that the Danish boxer recorded his impressions and later published them in his book, "My Life and My Fights. Twenty Years In The Ring." Nelson, whose real name was Ricard Christensen, fought some 240 times between 1905 and 1921. This is how he saw his tussle with Johnny Basham:

"Shortly after that (a fight with Jack Goldswain in London) I went to Liverpool Stadium, the largest arena I have fought in. Originally it had been a railway station and it was so big, that when you looked at it from the ring, which was in the centre of the arena, you could not distinguish one spectator from another in the back rows.

"The day I met England's best welterweight, Private Basham, the arena was completely sold out. Wherever I looked, there they were, standing shoulder-to-shoulder, their faces like small, white spots in the tobacco smoke.

"The applause which greeted Basham and myself was as huge as the arena itself and each succeeding round was greeted with the same amount of huge applause.

"Concerning the fight itself, I could have won it on a foul since Basham twice hit me too low. The second time the referee stopped the fight and asked me if I was able to continue. I said yes, much to the crowd's approval. But when I returned to my corner at the end of the round, my seconds berated me for agreeing to continue with the fight. "You fool," they said. "You could have won the fight on a foul," and yes, I suppose they were right, but since I never liked to win a fight in that way, I

told them to forget it — and as a result I lost the contest on points.

"The decision was okay, I suppose, but a couple of days later after my return to London, I received some very flattering letters, and some of them even made me the winner. I still have one of them. It goes like this:

"Thirty-Six Chapel Street,
Liverpool,
March 14th, 1914

Dear Sir,

Just a line to congratulate you on your display at the Stadium the other night. Frankly, I think Basham won by reason of his extra cleverness, but, at the same time, this was largely discounted by your skill in warding off several of his well aimed shots. Certainly you gave a splendid display and one which the spectators had every reason to be proud of. I am an Englishman and, naturally enough, am always anxious for Englishmen to win when they are up against other nationalities. In this case, however, I should have been delighted for you to win, not that I had anything against your opponent, but I was very struck with the very sportsmanlike way you extended your hand to Basham when he struck you low twice, although in fairness to him, I think it was unintentional. However you commanded my admiration when you shook his hand, and I was also pleased when you helped to pick him up after he had slipped down. You must remember that being a stranger the feelings of the crowd would be with Basham, but you made many friends. It is fair boxing, such as yours, that we want of and I would go a long way to see you box again.

May you always box the same way.

Yours, faithfully,
Robert H. Smith."

Mr. Smith may or may not have been present at Johnny's epic struggle with Gus Platts later that year at the Liverpool Stadium on Thursday, June 11th, 1914 but we can be fairly certain that he would have approved of the cleanness and openness of the bout. Johnny had only recently beaten Sid Stagg at the NSC in London, a win which entitled him to a tilt at Johnny Summers's British Welterweight title, and he could not afford to slip up against Platts.

Pudsey street was sold out and the paying customers were expecting a grand evening's entertainment. They were not disappointed. Hundreds were unable to get in and missed the thrilling contest. One of the enthralled spectators who did get in was Stephen Black, described by the

Gus Platts, the rugged Yorkshireman who fought Johnny four times

"Wrexham Advertiser" as "that well-known authority on boxing." Using his pen as effectively as Johnny Basham used his straight left, Black has left us with a fascinating account of that night's work:

"It was in the sixteenth round of a desperate battle that Johnny Basham, of Wrexham, revealed something akin to pugilistic greatness.

"This thrilling round ... brought out the extra reserve force of the ex-soldier, who, when apparently knocked-out, not only staved off the seemingly inevitable, but actually fought the rugged, untiring Yorkshireman to a standstill, so that he in turn appeared likely to go down for a count.

"Twenty hard and relentless rounds, fought out in the cleanest manner possible, by men whose liking for each other could be seen by their genial smile, who entered the ring in the best of tempers, and left it in the same manner. My only regret is that all the wrestling, win-at-any-cost fighters who have recently been very much in evidence were not there to see the contest.

"Ah! that sixteenth round! Down went Basham as he had never been seen to go before, and Platts of the chestnut hair and ruddy face, waited like a terrier for him to rise. Then at eight, when the Welshman weakly rose, the Tyke savagely went after him, and Liverpool held its breath. It had never seen Basham like this before, and it was very much afraid for its favourite.

"But Basham did everything but the usual or the obvious. He was expected to run or smother, but he stood up and fought. Platts going in to end a weakened man was greatly forced back, back, until anyone entering the Stadium at the time would have assumed Platts to be the finished and Basham the finisher. It was great boxing. When the round ended two minutes after the blow that had Basham to the floor the audience was in a frenzy of riotous admiration."

Johnny's late rally and the points lead he had built up in the earlier rounds were enough to bring him victory over a redoubtable opponent. As Stephen Black put it: *"It was a clean, open bout throughout, the men standing up to each other in fine style, and there was little of that tantalising holding and wrestling which are very often undesirable features of boxing contests."*

But if there was high drama at Liverpool and moments when true sportsmanship gladdened the heart of the real boxing fan — there was also humour and laughter, both of which were never very far away when Johnny Basham was around. On one memorable occasion, one of Johnny's fights was brought to a temporary halt not through any designs on Johnny's part, or those of his opponent, or, indeed through any actions of the referee, but because of some urchins on the roof of the Stadium. But let Johnny tell the story himself:

"It was in one of my contests in Liverpool, and Mr. Jack Smith was the third man in the ring. I won't mention my opponent; he will know all about it when he reads this.

"'The House Full' signs had been up long before we went into the ring, but you cannot keep kids from seeing a fight, and to get a peep of the battle some of those little Liverpool kids found their way across the neighbouring buildings on to the huge arched glass roof of the Stadium, and were risking their necks by lying flat on the glass covering and peering down at the ring, which must have been 70 or 80 feet below!

"We were well into our battle when there was a crash, a tinkle of glass and all eyes went to the roof!

"Get on with your boxing," growled Referee Smith, and, of course, being trained as a soldier, I jumped to obey orders, and scored one on the nose of my still staring opponent!

"A policeman was sent up to try and do something to scare away the kids, but nothing scared them, and before long we heard another crack, just like someone going through the ice on the pond. Following the crack came the funny scraping, sliding noise of a big lump of glass sliding down on the curved surface of that roof. We could hear every halt it made on its passage.

"It was evident that those kids were making the hole purposely for them to see through, for soon a piece of glass as big as a dinner plate, and nearly an inch thick, dropped in the ring, missing my head by about a foot! This was followed by a shower of smaller pieces of glass, and in spite of Mr. Smith telling us to box on I saw just the rear view of my opponent before he dodged through the ropes on the far side of the ring.

"Half the crowd were yelling at those kids and the other half bursting their sides laughing at my opponent diving for safety. But I mustn't crow, for when about four more lumps of glass hit that ring like lumps of boiler plate dropped from the top of the house, yours truly was under those ropes and looking for shelter as quick as ever he was when an air raid was on!"

Happy days! But the Liverpool Stadium was not all fun and frolic. It held its fair share of tragedy, too, as Johnny was to find to his cost...

CHAPTER IV

Death in the Ring

"I Am Very, Very Sorry;
He Must Have Been Out
Of Condition, Because
I Did Not Treat Him Harmfully."

By 1913 Johnny was beginning to make a name for himself in the world of boxing. The early reverses were forgotten as he swept from victory to victory. He was now confident enough to challenge the redoubtable Fred Welsh, but Welsh declined, saying he had already signed up for three twenty-round contests, and did not relish the prospect of a fourth.

Welsh or no Welsh, August started brightly for Johnny. On the twelfth of that month, he married Winifred Trader at the Roman Catholic Cathedral in Wrexham. But if August was to be a time of great happiness, it was also to be a time of great grief.

Nine days after Johnny's marriage, an event occurred which had the superstitious minded muttering darkly about the "thirteen" part of the year 1913. On August 21st of that year, the newly married Johnny Basham stepped into the ring at Liverpool and touched gloves with the South African, Harry Price. It was to be a fateful encounter, yet until the eleventh round, it had been a fairly unremarkable contest. It was in the eleventh round that Johnny sent Price to the boards for a count of nine. Slowly, the South African rose to his feet, looking "very groggy" and white. Johnny struck him again and, this time, Harry Price dropped to the boards where the back of his head made violent contact with the floor.

At once the injured man's seconds entered the ring and the referee awarded the fight to Basham, but to the dismay of all those present, Price failed to come round and, after being seen by a doctor, was taken by horse-drawn ambulance to the Liverpool Royal Infirmary. There was "considerable commotion" in the hall as Johnny held out his hands to his seconds. But before they could take off his gloves, two men "with policemen writtten all over their faces," stepped into the ring on either side of Johnny. *"If you don't mind, we'll take off those gloves,"* they said and they pushed aside the seconds who had begun to undo Johnny's gloves.

The two policemen took off the gloves and examined them thoroughly. Then they took off the hand bandages and inspected them minutely before wrapping them in paper and putting them into their pockets. The wondering and excited crowd could only gasp in disbelief as they saw the two police officers escort Johnny from the ring to his dressing room. There they sat whilst he dressed and then accompanied him to his hotel, the "Star and Garter." Even then, they followed him to the bathroom, and stood there while he had his bath and was rubbed down.

Johnny was then taken to the city's Dale-street Police Station, where he was charged with causing grievous bodily harm. Still numb and uncertain, Johnny made no reply when he was cautioned. He was given a couple of blankets and placed in a cell with two other men, drunks brought in earlier that night for fighting whilst under the influence of drink. Hardly the most sensitive treatment for a man whose whole world was threatening to cave in on him, but while Johnny paced his cell, wondering and waiting, frantic efforts were being made on his behalf.

His friends were trying desperately to obtain bail but were told that this might be difficult, as the Chief Constable was out of town. The same reply was given to Mr. James Fairrie, one of the biggest sugar merchants in the country, and a director of the Liverpool Stadium. He went to the police station in person, asking for Johnny to be released, but to no avail. For the first time in his life, Johnny would have to spend the night in a prison cell.

Sleep was, of course, out of the question. Back and forth, back and forth, Johnny paced the confines of his cell, wondering what on earth was going to happen to him and, no doubt, wondering how things were with Harry Price. He wrapped himself in his blankets and tried to doze, but sleep simply would not come. At last, about 7.30 the next morning, the spy-hole in the cell door opened and a voice called out, *"Basham, come here a minute! I want you."* As Johnny came nearer, the voice continued, *"I don't want to scare you, but Harry Price is dead."*

As he heard these words, Johnny would not have been human if thoughts of the gallows and the hangman's rope had not flashed through his mind but, terribly upset, he only said, *"I am very, very sorry; he must have been out of condition, because I did not treat him harmfully."*

Half an hour later, Johnny was brought from his cell and allowed to sit in the charge room, talking to the police until the court opened at 11.30. Mr. Fairrie had continued his efforts on Johnny's behalf that morning and had managed to retain the services of the well-known

Liverpool solicitor, Mr. Benn, who snatched a few words with the boxer before they both entered the court. Inside the court, Johnny was spared the ordeal of standing in the dock, and was instead shepherded by one of the policemen to the well of the court, where he stood next to the solicitor's table. Mr. Benn duly asked for bail, and Mr. Harvey Duder, the prosecuting solicitor, applied for a remand till the following Tuesday, on a bail of £100.

This was granted and Johnny moved towards the door but a policeman blocked his way. Taking him to a window, the policeman pointed to the vast crowd gathered outside.

"You would never get out, Johnny," he said. "They would all want to either shake your hand, pat your back, or tell you how sorry they are, and they would never let you get away, so we must smuggle you out somehow."

And so Johnny was taken to a little door at the back of the court and then let out with a friend of his, a man who had been told by the police to show him the way to the pier.

"So many twists and twirls were there that I don't think I could ever find that way again. Never mind, we got to the pier all right and took one of the ferry boats to Birkenhead, the Cheshire side of the river, and from there we went by hired car to Wrexham, and although my friend joked and tried to cheer me upon the journey, Johnny Basham was a very thoughtful fellow indeed."

At Wrexham a great crowd had gathered to welcome Johnny back. He was home again and out of police custody but, on Monday, August 25th, 1913 the Liverpool Deputy Coroner opened the inquest on Harry Price. Johnny did not attend the proceedings which were mainly of a formal character. The court, in Liverpool's Dale-street, heard James W. Harris, described as a manager and trainer of boxers, identify the body and reveal that the dead man's real name was Isidore Price ("Issy" to his mother). Price's parents lived in South Africa and Harris had cabled them in Pietermaritzburg, informing them of their son's death. Price had been a healthy, temperate young man of about twenty years of age who had come to England to further his career in professional boxing.

The next day, Harry Price was buried. Originally, it had been intended to bury him in Liverpool's Moreton Cemetery but, once it was learned he was Jewish, these plans were changed and it was decided to bury him in Liverpool's Jewish burial ground, Thomas Drive, Broadgreen. Johnny, Mr. Arnold Wilson, the referee on that fatal night, Mr. Fairrie and several well-known Liverpool sportsmen were present at the funeral. It began with a short preliminary service at the synagogue of which Johnny would write almost sixteen years later:

"A very curious incident occurred which will always live in my memory. This happened during the burial service in the synagogue. The service was read in the Jewish language, and at one particular part, everybody in that synagogue who was a Hebrew turned right round and looked at me. I couldn't have felt more uncomfortable, and they all stood up, and pointed their fingers at me."

After this service the body was taken by train from Liverpool's Lime-street station. The Liverpool Rabbi officiated at the funeral and, as the coffin was lowered, one man in particular felt the loss keenly:

"It gave me a funny feeling to see that coffin being lowered into the grave, but I was at least clear in my conscience that everything I had done could bear the strictest investigation."

Harry Price had been buried but investigations still continued into the manner of his death. On September 4th, the inquest re-opened. James Harris, known as "Jim The Penman," because of his willingness to enter into "newspaper warfare" with anyone who dared to criticise his boxers, told the court that he had been Price's trainer for three years. Price was strong and healthy and had boxed in America and Canada. He was the Welter and Middleweight Champion of South Africa.

Price had boxed at Liverpool on August 7th and lost on points, but he had given so "excellent a show" that he was immediately booked to fight Johnny Basham on August 21st. He was to receive £60 for his efforts — win, lose or draw. The fight would be over fifteen rounds and six ounce gloves would be used. On the day of the fight the South African was in perfect training and physical condition and in good spirits. Both Basham and Price had been good friends and there was absolutely no suggestion of any ill-feeling between them.

Harris went on to say that, until the tenth round, neither man could claim to hold the advantage. He had never seen a cleaner contest and the referee had been given no cause to caution either of them for fouls or rule infringements. Nor did either of the two boxers show any external signs of injury. Between the tenth and eleventh rounds, he had spoken to Price who told him that he thought he was winning the fight. Price told his trainer that he was going to make the next round a fast one and started briskly. Then came the fatal blow. The doctor tried to revive Harry Price but without success. When asked how much Johnny Basham would receive for the fight, Harris replied that the Welshman would be paid £50 for winning and £40 if he were defeated.

The next witness to be called was Dr. O'Connor who had been

present at the ringside. He confirmed that the fight had been clean and fair. Price had been well trained and fit and there were no signs of any chest or heart trouble. He had fallen through getting his legs crossed. Before taking him to the infirmary Dr. O'Connor had injected Price with strychnine.

James Fairrie, sugar refiner and chairman of the Stadium Company, and other witnesses then testified that the fight had been clean and fair. They thought that the referee had acted properly throughout the contest and at no time had there been any occasion for him to stop the fight.

The referee, Mr. Arnold Wilson, was himself a director of the Stadium and a man with some five years experience of boxing. He told the inquest that there had been no ill blood between the two men, nor was there any hint of anything underhand or foul. He had been chosen by Basham and Price after some initial disagreement between them over the choice of referee. Of the rounds fought, he had scored 41 to Basham and 39 to Price. As he had said, the fight had been absolutely fair. No blow had been strong enough to injure either man. When he gave the signal for the boxers to resume, Harry Price had come up quite strongly. After the first knockdown, the South African champion had risen to his feet, but his legs had crossed. Basham had come forward and simply pushed his opponent, who fell heavily. It was true to say that Price had been something of an unknown quality for the Liverpool boxing public.

The next man to give evidence was John Arthur Dean, the timekeeper, who had served in that capacity for forty years. He had seen nothing foul in the fight. He thought Basham the cleverer man and Price the stronger. When he counted "nine," Price jumped up and smiled at him. Basham then approached slowly and caught Price on the chin. He staggered and fell heavily on the back of his head.

Dean's evidence was supported by Arthur Campbell, a soldier, who had been the master of ceremonies. George Rodell, one of Price's seconds, said he followed Price carefully and would not have allowed him to box if he had not been fit. He did not consider the knockout blow to be a severe one. When he got back to his feet in the eleventh round, Rodell thought that Price was quite strong enough to complete the fifteen rounds.

All this time Johnny Basham had been watching and listening, listening to the evidence being sifted and re-sifted, to the rules of boxing being dissected in minute detail, to the many varying accounts of the fateful happenings of that August night. He was not called upon to give evidence himself, although quite willing to do so, but after what had already been said, his solicitor saw no useful purpose in calling his client to the stand.

Years later, however, Johnny was to re-live the events of that dreadful night in the columns of the "Empire News." As he saw it, the tragedy unfolded in this way:

"About the ninth round I thought I saw Harry falter in his stride, and so I speeded up a bit, with the result that I was getting more on top of my man when the tenth round came along, but I was far from having things my own way, for just a few seconds before the tenth round ended Price dug up a reserve of strength from somewhere and tore at me like a tiger.

"'Watch him this round,' said my seconds as I sat in my corner. ' I think you are wrong,' I said, ' as I think that last spurt took a lot out of him. Anyhow, I am going to see what he is made of as soon as this round opens.'

"Someone must have thought the same as me, for as the bell clanged for the opening of the eleventh round someone near the ringside yelled: ' Go on, get him, Johnny, you have him licked!' Price looked anything but licked as he came up from his stool, for it was he who started out to make the fighting and not me. A right hand loaded with high explosives was only avoided by a quick shift on my part, and then I pulled myself together and went in to do my job.

"He turned quickly, wild at having missed. I hit him with a a left hand full in the face, and stepping in as soon as my left had connected I smashed a right hand to his chin.

"Everything I had was in that punch, and down went the South African. Game as a terrier, he started to climb up at eight, and was on his feet at nine. Just a quick feint to his stomach and down came his hands. Once again I banged my right to his chin, and down he went, this time he faced the canvas spreadeagled on the floor.

"I walked to my corner. The referee started to count. Those seconds seemed the longest I had ever heard in my life."

Although Johnny was not required to testify, several other witnesses confirmed that Price had had his legs crossed just before he fell and that Basham's blow had not been an unduly severe one. Dr. Fisher of the Liverpool Royal Infirmary stated that the hospital's medical staff had worked throughout the night to try and save the life of Harry Price, but he died during the early hours of the morning, without ever once having regained consciousness. Price had died from the laceration of a very important part of the brain and there was haemorrhage at the back of the pleura. There were no signs of Price having been roughly knocked about.

After hearing evidence from John Henry Thwaites, a member of the National Sporting Club, and the original choice for referee, and listening to the Deputy Coroner's summing-up, the jury retired for three-quarters of an hour. The verdict, read out by their Foreman, was that

"The jury are agreed that it was a boxing match and that death was caused by misadventure, but the jury strongly protest against the practice of the knock out blow counting as a win."

Johnny Basham was then brought before Mr. R.J. Ward in the second Police Court. Mr. Duder, representing the police, referred to the verdict of the coroner's jury and, offering no evidence against Basham, asked for him to be released. Looking straight at Basham, the Judge said,

"To me, this has been a clean, boxing contest, conducted on proper lines by two men who have boxed in a proper sporting manner. It may just have happened to you as to the unfortunate man who has been killed. You are discharged."

And with that Johnny left the court to be very warmly greeted by his friends and followers. In fact he had to submit to:

"having my back slapped that much that I was tender for weeks, before I got out of that court-room. But that was nothing to the job I had to get free of the court itself, as the crowds would simply not go away, and it took me a full hour to get a distance that I could have walked ordinarily in ten minutes."

At last Johnny's long ordeal was over. Now he had to pick up the pieces of his shattered career and start again. Should he have retired from the ring after Price's death? Tragic as the affair was, Johnny had fought a good, clean fight and he had nothing to blame himself for. The stadium doctor had examined Price on the night of the fight and found him to be a well-trained, muscular man, well above the average. Indeed, until his fatal meeting with Johnny, Harry Price had never been knocked out.

So should Johnny have quit the fight game? Price was not the first man to have died as a result of fatal injuries received in the ring — between December 6th, 1897 and April 24th, 1901, four men died from the effects of blows received at the National Sporting Club alone — nor, sadly, would he be the last. Boxing was Johnny's profession, he knew no other. He must have searched the depths of his soul but in the end he boxed on.

But he did not set foot inside a boxing ring for almost two months. This scarcely sounds like a long time, but it must be remembered that Johnny had already fought no less than eleven men in 1913. By the time

Scotsman Eddie Beattie,
Johnny's first opponent after the tragic death of Harry Price.

he met Price, he had been fighting practically at the rate of one contest a month, so that, by the standards of the time, it was quite a long lay-off.

He did withdraw from the planned fight with Tom McCormick at the Cosmo Gymnasium in Plymouth, but whatever the strength of his real feelings on the Harry Price affair — and he referred to it as that "stark and terrible tragedy that kept me awake for nights, and made me for a while wish I had never seen a boxing ring." — he was back at his beloved Liverpool Stadium on Thursday, October 16th, 1913.

The question was: How would Johnny react to his new opponent, Eddie Beattie? How would he face the ordeal of returning to the place where "a very gentlemanly and unassuming young fellow" had been tragically struck down? Whatever Johnny's feelings may have been, he must have been encouraged by the wonderful reception the Liverpool boxing fans gave him. They cheered him to the echo and he more than repaid them with a brilliant tactical display and a victory on points over fifteen rounds. There are those who say that Johnny was inclined to pull his punches after what happened to Harry Price, but if that was the case, there was no sign of it that night against Eddie Beattie, who occupied the opposite corner on Johnny's return to the ring.

Johnny piled into the Newcastle on Tyne based Scotsman, flooring him no less than five times, four of those in the third round, before finally clinching an outstanding points victory in the fifteenth round. Pudsey street was ecstatic. "Liverpool's Own" had thrown off the traumas of the past few months and re-instated his claim to be one of the very best welterweights in the country.

Johnny Basham never forgot Harry Price. Years later, on his return to Newport, he would spend time training the young boxing hopefuls of the town, one of whom was Mr. John Lannen. Mr. Lannen still remembers vividly the times he spent sparring with Johnny and recalls the old champion telling him never to punch anyone really hard and to hold his punches back. The death of Harry Price did not stop Johnny from continuing his boxing career and it did not prevent him from recording some notable triumphs, but always at the back of his mind perhaps, the sight of Harry Price, cross-legged, and dropping to the canvas must have been with him.

CHAPTER V

The National Sporting Club

"I Was Congratulated
By A Large Number Of
The Members Of The Club
On My Brilliant Show."

Professional boxing has its roots in the days of the old bare-knuckle fighters. Men like Jem Mace and Daniel Mendoza, the champions of old, literally fought their opponents to a standstill. In such fights, stamina and sheer strength were often more important than pure boxing skill, as it was the ability to take and give punches and, above all, remain on one's feet, no matter how hard and gruelling the fight, that was the mark of a true champion.

Not surprisingly, the authorities took a dim view of such affairs. They were often clandestine contests, held at a secret location and ready to move on at a moment's notice. Lookouts were posted to give warning of any impending police moves to stop the fights. If the police heard about these bouts, they wasted no time in breaking them up. These were the "professional" fights where the men inside the makeshift ring had their "backers" whilst, among the spectators, money changed hands freely as bets were taken.

These bare-knuckle fist fights were also the norm in the valleys of South Wales. Any slight difference of opinion, any long-standing grudge was likely to be settled with bare fists on the nearest mountain side. Often death was the end result. There have been cases where one of the two men fighting insisted on continuing the fight even though it was obvious to all concerned that he had no hope of winning, and even though his opponent was willing to stop.

There was usually only one outcome in such cases: battered and bleeding, and very near to death, the loser was spirited away, only to die later in some lonely farm house or miner's cottage. Gradually, however, sanity began to prevail. Reforms were made and steps were taken to secure the safety of those boxing professionally. A limit was placed on the number of rounds any two men could fight. Gloves began to be used and, slowly but surely, the old bare knuckle fights became a thing of the past. Doctors were present at the ringside and soon it became unnecessary to stand in an open field or on the side of a mountain to watch a prize-fight.

As interest in boxing grew in the 1890s, halls and clubs were built where spectators could watch the proceedings in comfort. The premier and the most famous of all these clubs was the National Sporting Club in Covent Garden. At its London Headquarters, the club stood for "manly," "scientific" and skilful boxing. Fair play and courage in adversity were other virtues the members of the club admired. (In all these respects, Johnny Basham and the Club were at one. The Association between the two would turn out to be a "marriage made in Heaven.")

Despite a rather poor start when it was rocked by a series of scandals, the club began to develop the leading role in British boxing which it had until the formation of the British Boxing Board of Control in 1929.

This leading role was immeasurably strengthened when its first president, Lord Lonsdale, who held the position for thirty-eight years, was persuaded to put up the first Lonsdale Belts for British title holders. If a champion succeeded in defending the belt three times, it automatically became his own personal property, together with a small life pension at the age of fifty. To ensure that the NSC kept its hold on British boxing, the belts were only awarded for contests held within the precincts of the Club itself.

The firm of Mappin and Webb was instructed to design the belts at a cost, in those days, of some £250 each. The first man to wear one round his waist was Pontypridd's Freddie Welsh who defeated Johnny Summers at the NSC in November, 1909.

The new Lonsdale Belts put an end to the confusion which had sometimes prevailed as to who exactly was the real title holder. Henceforth the Lonsdale Belt holder was the champion at his weight and soon it became every boxer's burning ambition to become the proud owner of one of Lord Lonsdale's Belts.

In this respect, at least, Johnny Basham was no different to his fellow boxers and, by 1914, he was ready to make his challenge for the British Welterweight Title held by Johnny Summers. But first he had to dispose of Sid Stagg.

Stagg, a Londoner from Deptford, had been out to Australia, where, although he did not exactly carry all before him, he had won a few fights and was reported to have improved not only in physique, but also in cleverness. A match was accordingly made between Johnny and Stagg for £50 a side and a National Sporting Club purse of £250. The fight aroused a tremendous amount of interest in the Wrexham area and the local paper, the "Wrexham Advertiser" dispatched its reporter to question Johnny Basham. It turned out to be a revealing interview.

The "Advertiser's" man on the spot began by saying: *"I found not the generally conceived type of pugilist with the husky voice, the battered nose and the cauliflower ear, but a healthy, clean featured young fellow, bubbling over with youthful spirits and affability itself."*

He went on to speak to Johnny's then trainer and manager, Sergeant Henderson of the Royal Welch Fusiliers, who told him that Johnny required very little training. *"The life he leads keeps him fit," he added "and Basham is not one of those men who departs from his regular habits directly after a big fight. He is always the same and no one need worry about his condition."*

Johnny himself told the reporter: *"Wrexham people are taking a very kindly interest in my career and I am now one of them."* The conversation then continued:

REPORTER: *But you are a South Walian?*

BASHAM: *I was born there, but I am a Wrexham man now and have got very fond of the place. I have settled down here and intend to make it my home as long as I live.*

REPORTER: *To come to the point, how do you feel for next Monday's bout?*

BASHAM: *As fit as a fiddle, I never felt better in my life.*

REPORTER: *What is your general course of training?*

BASHAM: *Early to bed and early to rise is one thing. Between breakfast and dinner I take a brisk walk about the town, and in the afternoon I run to Bangor and back, a distance of ten miles. In the evening I come down the rooms and have a good time with my boys and having given them a lesson or two I have a good set-to myself with my sparring partners.*

REPORTER: *Do you take intoxicants at all?*

BASHAM: *No, I am very careful as to that, I am a total abstainer, and the only thing I indulge in is a cigarette, and then only when I have nothing on.*

REPORTER: *What do you think of your chances for next Monday?*

BASHAM: *I never think anything about losing, you know. I always feel I am going to win, and if I lose it will only be after I have done my best.*

The Stagg versus Basham fight took place on Monday, April 27th, 1914 over fifteen rounds at the National Sporting Club. It was the first time that Johnny had boxed in London and he was surprised to see that the "Club" had its own way of doing things:

"One thing struck me as being very strange. That was the fact that the referee operated from a chair ***outside*** *the ring whereas all my fights had been with the referee* ***in the ring*** *with myself and my opponent!"*

Johnny weighed in at ten stone four pounds whilst his opponent tipped the scales at ten stones five and a half pounds. Johnny had, of course, prepared at Wrexham whilst Stagg had trained at the Nag's Head, Welling, Kent. As they stepped into the ring before a very large audience, including many of Johnny's followers from Wales and the North of England, both men looked in the peak of condition.

They were well matched for height but Stagg was the older of the two and looked his one and a half pounds heavier. Johnny impressed with his speed and footwork but Stagg defended stolidly. By the halfway mark, Johnny was ahead on points but Stagg was not an easy man to score against. The fight was hardly spectacularly exciting for the paying customers, but Johnny was trying his hardest to bring it to a swift conclusion, more than once aiming a right swing at Stagg's head, but the Deptford man successfully avoided the worst of these. In the end, however, the Welshman was a worthy winner on points.

Reviewing the fight later, one well-known sporting writer thought that Basham might be the greatest welterweight in the world, but he would like to see him against a man who had the speed and ability to try and rush him. Basham, he continued, had a really good left hand, a snappy, if not too forceful right, while his defence is very close to perfection.

"He can avoid with real cleverness, provided that he can escape being bustled. He stands up straight when he wants to cover, and guards his ribs and stomach in almost hermetic fashion with his forearms and elbows. And in this respect, he stands well ahead of the average hermit-crab opponent. Stagg may be, and undoubtedly is, a tough man. The Deptford boy has improved amazingly since and during his Australian trip, but he is still far too slow. Basham got off well with left leads to the face and fierce digs from the same hand to the body, and Stagg waited. For though he spurted at times and promised all sorts of things, the rounds were ticked off with steady increase to Basham's lead. The private was forcing matters, and kept forcing them. Stagg got away and would feint rather cleverly, and would later dig quite respectably, but he was always being out-paced and out-generalled. He was waiting for something apparently, and was content to continue waiting, until he discovered that he had been

The young Sergeant Basham

waiting too long — and then he hadn't the reserve speed left to bustle Basham."

Meanwhile the (unnamed) "Wrexham Advertiser" reporter was in danger of becoming a frequent visitor to the Basham household. Hardly had the boxer returned to Wrexham than the editor had dispatched his man once again, this time anxious to hear the story of the fight from Private Basham's own lips.

"From his appearance one would never imagine that he had been engaged in a tussle, fraught with such importance. He bore not the slightest trace of injury, and one would gather, from the conversation, that he enjoyed the occasion much the same as if he had been on a holiday trip. He alluded, in fact, to the pleasure he derived in witnessing the English Cup Final on Saturday and in seeing the many and varied sights of the great city.

"What is your own impression of the contest?" our representative asked, anxious to get to the point.

BASHAM: *I expected to get a hard fight, but it proved to be a much easier job altogether than I anticipated.*

REPORTER: *I notice that while all the critics are unanimous as to your great superiority, some of them seemed to expect a little bit more from you.*

BASHAM: *The reason was, that I had no chance of showing my powers. I boxed the best way I could with a man who would not fight. If a man won't open out and fight, you cannot possibly show your best. He simply covered up and was hanging on for a knockout.*

REPORTER: *Then although you were compelled to box him before you could meet the champion you don't think he is the best man you have met?*

BASHAM: *Not by a long way, in fact it was the easiest contest I have had for a long time.*

REPORTER: *Then you were never in much danger?*

BASHAM: *Not at all. I had to keep forcing the fighting from beginning to end, but he would not let himself go, and covered so much that I could only use my right about four times.*

REPORTER: *What sort of reception did you get?*

BASHAM: *A very nice one indeed, both at the beginning and the end, and I was congratulated by a large number of the members of the Club on my brilliant show and upon the way I had outpointed my opponent.*

REPORTER: *How do you stand now with regard to Summers, the champion? Is there any truth in the rumour that you have to meet Matt Wells first?*

BASHAM: *Wells is not in the country, whereas Summers landed from Australia on Tuesday and has issued a challenge in which he is prepared to meet the winner of the Basham-Stagg fight.*

REPORTER: *I suppose you are accepting?*

BASHAM: *I have already left my deposit with the "Sportsman" to bind the match, so that it is sure to come off now.*

REPORTER: *And what are your prospects?*

BASHAM: *Very good, I think. I was told in London I ought to be the holder of the belt on my form.*

REPORTER: *Did Stagg appear to be satisfied with the result?*

BASHAM: *Yes, he is a very good sport, and while we were having a bath together afterwards he remarked: "You are a better lad than I am, Basham. I never met a man as fast as you. When I started thinking which way you were coming you were on me in no time. You were too fast and clever for me."*

The "Advertiser's" representative concluded his report by saying: *"And now the sports of Wrexham are all anxiously awaiting the great championship contest. It is certain Private Basham will have the good wishes of hundreds of his fellow townsmen in his venture and should the Belt be brought to Wrexham his reception is bound to be a great one."*

What the unknown reporter did not say was that the Stagg fight was, amazingly, near enough Johnny's sixty-seventh appearance in the ring. Early records are confusing and, sometimes, downright contradictory but there seems little doubt that Johnny had fought at least sixty times before he won the right to face Johnny Summers — and this is not counting exhibition bouts and the number of times he fought in boxing booths. Add to this the countless rounds of sparring he must have done and it becomes clear that his was a very long apprenticeship indeed, especially when compared to most modern-day fighters. The man who would enter the ring against Johnny Summers at the National Sporting Club on December 14th, 1914 was an experienced campaigner, despite his comparative youth. Glory, and the Lonsdale Belt, was there for the taking. What was more, he now had a family to provide for, Winifred Basham having given birth to a baby daughter, Betty, back in August. More than most men, Johnny literally held his future in his own two hands. Would he seize the opportunity?

CHAPTER VI
Taking the Belt

"Then I Let One Go With All The Strength In My Body."

On the day of the Summers fight, a friend asked Johnny what he intended to eat before going into the ring. Johnny could not make up his mind between fish and chicken, but the "friend" in question recommended a "good fat juicy steak, for by the way Summers looked at you, you'll have no teeth to chew steak with when this fight is over".

As it happened, Johnny did not order steak but his friend's words were to prove oddly prophetic. Johnny himself had no illusions about the size of the task facing him. There was no doubt in his, or anyone else's mind, that Johnny Summers was a very tough customer indeed. Born in Middlesborough, the champion had been raised in London's Canning Town. In his time, he had claimed both the British Featherweight championship and the British Lightweight title. He had been defeated by, amongst others, Freddy Welsh and Jim Driscoll, but he was nothing if not determined and in June, 1912 he took the British Welterweight title from Arthur Evernden.

It was this title which the newly promoted Sergeant Johnny Basham intended to make his own. Himself a Catholic, he was now taking on another, very devout Roman Catholic in the person of Johnny Summers. Every time he entered the ring, Summers would put a small crucifix inside his sock. At the start of each round he went down on one knee and made the Sign of The Cross.

Summers had been boxing professionally since the age of seventeen. With or without divine help, he had already carved two notches on the Lonsdale Belt and only needed to beat Basham to make it his own. He had trained for the fight at Shoeburyness, where he spent a lot of time boxing with the soldiers, and allowing the biggest and best of them to punch his jaw as often and as hard as they liked. Eventually, he grew so confident in the powers of his chin to withstand punishment, that he came to believe that nobody could knock him out, least of all Sergeant Johnny Basham. Nor was he alone in this belief. One member of the NSC was so sure Summers was going to win that he placed a £300 bet on him.

Johnny Summers made the fatal mistake of underestimating Johnny Basham's punching power.

In fact, Summers was most people's favourite. He had fought in Australia and America and was more experienced than Basham. Arrangements had already been made to photograph him holding the Belt as soon as the fight was over. By then, or so it was thought, the Belt would be his to keep, and he would have earned himself the pension of a pound a week for life at the age of fifty which went with the permanent ownership of the belt.

The fight was scheduled to last twenty rounds. "Flaxen-haired" Johnny Summers stood only five feet five inches and was giving away height to Basham, who was five feet eight and a half inches. The Welshman was the first into the ring, accompanied by his seconds and Summers soon followed. The referee, Mr. J. H. Douglas, quickly laid down the law to both men:

"You will protect yourself at all times. I do not waste my time, your time, or annoy the members of the club by yelling constantly "break," so I warn you, and if no notice is taken of that warning — Out Goes The Offender!"

Then it was down to business. The first round started badly for Basham. Watched by the packed club, and the serried ranks of starched white shirts, he was made to miss so many times by Summers that he looked like a regular novice. But if the first round was bad for the Welshman, then the second was worse, much worse. Fifteen years later, in a series of articles he wrote for the "Empire News," Basham described what happened:

"I had stuck several fast left hands into his face and was very pleased with my work. Johnny had kept poking out his chin, inviting my left hand, in the hope of getting a good whack back at me, but I was over-reaching him and was scoring without any returns when like a bolt from a clear sky came his answer. I had sent a left hand across, expecting as usual to connect on Johnny's mouth or nose, but this time Johnny swerved sharp to his right, letting my left fist pass over his left shoulder, and at the same time reaching me on the mouth with a vicious left hook that nearly tore my head from my shoulders."

It was a peach of a punch and it sent Basham just where Summers wanted him — down onto the boards. Down went Basham and Summers must have felt that the Belt and pension were his. But Basham got up. It was all he could do to get up at the count of nine, but somehow he did and then he rallied as best as he could, clinched desperately and held on. He had been within an inch of the defeat Summers's supporters had so confidently predicted. But then, from the brink of disaster, he hauled himself back and from the third round onwards, it was the "Fighting Fusilier" who began to get the upper hand. As the "Sporting Life's" reporter put it:

"Basham won in absolutely decisive style. For two rounds he had rather a bad time; for the next six he boxed with real artistry, his methods being a happy combination of speed in attack and puzzling defence; then in the final round he did what few even of his own supporters believed him capable of doing, landed a punch that was hard enough and true enough to knock out any welterweight in the world."

It was a heavy right on Summers's jaw that did for the Londoner. Caught by surprise, he dropped and did not get up again until the referee was counting "nine". When he did manage to rise, it was an easy job for Basham to finish him off and ensure the Belt would go to Wales. There was to be no life pension for Johnny Summers at the age of fifty.

Yet in the eyes of many, Summers had put on one of the best boxing displays of his life. The well respected referee, Eugene Corri, certainly thought so. He was convinced that Summers had never boxed better than he did against Basham. His fatal mistake was to underestimate the Welshman. Heedless of the risks he was taking, he deliberately went out of his way to offer Basham the point of his jaw and suffered the consequences in the ninth.

After the fight, Johnny Basham summed up his tactics which had proved so successful:

"It was part of my game not to hit him too hard with the right hand, because I did not want to let him know that I had a right. He fell into the trap which I laid for him, and pushed his jaw out purposely to be hit. Then I let one go with all the strength in my body. It took effect and knocked him down. He got up again in a very groggy state, and I immediately sent out another right-hander to the jaw, which knocked him down, this time not to get up again."

Summers could only reflect ruefully:

"I thought I had got Basham. I did not think he had a punch. I took too many risks. We live and learn, but I ought to have learned long ago not to go so far out of my way to look for trouble."

Basham had been given a "special dispensation" by his officers to train for the Summers fight, and they must have been well pleased at the reflected glory his victory had brought to the regiment. There was no doubting the feelings of the citizens of Wrexham. When Johnny returned to the town he was given a hero's welcome. The Band of The Royal Welch Fusiliers turned out to head the procession as the new Lonsdale

Belt holder was carried shoulder high through the streets of the small North Wales town, the cheers of a large, appreciative crowd ringing in his ears.

Two days later, a reporter from the "Wrexham Advertiser" called at the Sergeant's Whitegate Road home. Acknowledging that he had had to fight for his success, Johnny said that he *"felt the utmost confidence all through, but there was no play about it."* As for the second round, he told the reporter that it was a mistake to think he had been badly hurt.

"I was never touched on the point at all. During my training some of my teeth were loosened, and Summers caught me in the mouth and caused me a good deal of pain. I was in a little trouble, but nothing to speak of, and I never felt like "going down" the least bit. There was not a moment in the fight when I felt like getting beat."

In response to the reporter's questioning, Johnny told how he had deliberately set out to lure Summers into the trap which proved to be the Londoner's undoing:

"Yes, I really led Summers into a trap. He refused to open out at all, but covered up continually and was all in-fighting. I gave him some punishment, however, and in the fourth round split his nose open with a left. However, it was no use of forcing it and I altered my tactics. I boxed him in my best style and tapped and tapped away so long that he got the idea I had no power left. He then opened out, and decided to take my blows with the object of replying with heavier ones, but the moment he gave me a chance I took it. The "point" was left open and I crashed him a right-hander which surprised him and his friends and settled the fight."

And those teeth? In 1929, in his "Empire News" reminiscences, Johnny recalled how, whether loosened in training or not, it was Summers's second round punch that made him and them part company:

"Up to this time, I had boasted of a set of teeth that would have served well for any dentifrice advertisement, but I am sorry to say that that is where my teeth and I went our various ways! Some were scattered about the ring, one or two went in the sawdust tub, one I spat out as I fell, and I am thundering sure I swallowed a couple."

As he contemplated the future, however, Sergeant Johnny Basham would not have felt too down-hearted about the loss of a few teeth. He was now the Welterweight Champion of Great Britain and the man to beat. The Lonsdale belt was his to defend. Two more victories and it would be his outright. The only thing marring his victory was his country's involvement in a great European war. How would this affect his boxing future? As he told the correspondent of the "Wrexham

Advertiser," *"The NSC is now closed for the season and there will be no contests for some time. But you must remember I am not a civilian now. I am a soldier, and I want to do my best for my country. I am ready to go when called upon."*

War or no war, Johnny made his first defence of his new title on May 10th, 1915. His chosen opponent was Sergeant Tom McCormick of the Manchester Regiment. McCormick was something of an oddity, having taught himself to box through reading books by the likes of Jim Driscoll and then practising the moves in a mirror. But there was nothing odd about the way in which he beat Johnny Summers in one round in Australia to claim the British and Commonwealth titles. Flushed with success, he then went one better, defeating Denmark's Waldemar Holberg to claim the world crown. These titles were then taken away from him on points by Matt Wells, but on his return to Britain after the outbreak of war, he seemed a logical choice to challenge Johnny Basham for his newly acquired Lonsdale Belt.

Irish-born McCormick had started his professional career in April, 1911 and he and Johnny Basham had met once before, the match ending in a draw. Much was, therefore, expected of the Irishman as he weighed in at ten stone and four-and-a-half pounds. The fight was a scheduled twenty-rounder for £100 a side, plus the NSC purse and the Lonsdale Belt, and the betting was six to four on Basham, who had tipped the scales at ten stone five pounds.

As the fight progressed, McCormick proved to be a huge disappointment for his followers. He was made to look woefully slow by Basham who danced around him "shooting out his left at a remarkable pace." For round after round this same pattern continued — with Johnny showing no signs of slacking as he buzzed round his opponent like a demented bee, whilst all McCormick could do was to cover up. It was clear that the Irishman was outclassed and the beginning of the end came when, in the twelfth, a "stinging left" from Basham sent his opponent to the ropes.

He was saved by the bell, but in the very next round, a succession of two-handed blows dropped him to the floor. At this point Johnny almost blotted his copy-book by standing over his opponent ready to strike. *"A shout of warning from his corner, however, brought him to a sense of the fitness of things, and he held his hand until McCormick was up."* He did not have very long to wait for, shortly afterwards, the referee stopped the fight. The second notch on the Lonsdale Belt had been cut. Tom McCormick later went with his regiment to France where, sadly, he was

Johnny Basham proudly wears the Lonsdale Belt he made his own.

killed in action in 1916.

One more successful defence and the coveted belt would be Johnny's. But he had to wait another year before the chance came. This time the fight was against Scots boxer, Eddie Beattie, another man Johnny had met before, and beaten, in Liverpool. For this second defence, the NSC offered a purse of £475. Beattie had trouble making the weight, but tore into Johnny from the opening bell, showering blows upon the champion. It seemed as if the tenacious Glaswegian would wear Johnny down with his bull-like rushes, but Basham boxed skilfully on the retreat and waited for Eddie to tire himself out:

"I had experienced these wild fellows before, and a rushing boxer is for all the world like a trout that is being played by an expert angler. He has to be allowed to tire himself before he is ready to tackle. Of course, there is one big difference in this comparison, and that is that during the tiring process the trout cannot hit back!"

Until the tenth, Beattie's bulldog strength kept him in the fight, but after that it was all Johnny Basham. He easily eluded Beattie's wild and clumsy rushes and, in the sixteenth, landed three or four blows in the Scotsman's face without reply. By now Johnny was streets ahead on points and boxing with ever increasing confidence. The confidence was justified when, in the nineteenth round, the champion knocked the challenger down twice and the referee stepped in to put an end to the fight:

"And so I was the winner of my third belt contest. The Lord Lonsdale Challenge Belt was my own property, and I had won all my three belt contests by the knock-out route. Not bad, this, for a man who was rated as a clever boxer, but not by any means a knocker-out.

"All Wales went wild when the news got through that the Lonsdale Belt was to stay in the Principality. I was met on my arrival and could have had anything I liked to ask for. My officers told me that I had done a great thing for the Royal Welch Fusiliers, and for many a long day after my win over Eddie Beattie I had what was known in the army as "cushy days.""

What Johnny, in his modesty, neglected to say was that he was the first man to win a Lonsdale Belt outright at his particular weight. From now on, whatever else happened, he was a part of Welsh and British boxing history, assured of his own little niche in the annals of his sport.

CHAPTER VII

In which Johnny goes to War

"Time And Time Again We Would Make Long Journeys In The Night In Order To Box An Exhibition For Some Of The Boys Who Had Been Wounded."

There were no arias being sung at the London Opera House on March 22nd, 1915. Nor were the chief performers on the stage that night the usual prima donnas or operatic tenors. They were two gladiators of the roped square — Johnny Basham and Matt Wells — and their meeting, in the luxurious surroundings of the Opera House, was the first time an outside promoter had organised a big "spectacular" since Europe had exploded into war almost eight months before.

Matt Wells already held a decision over Johnny, having k.o'd him in Swansea at the end of December, 1912 but the Johnny Basham he now faced was an altogether different proposition. In fact the new Johnny was so good that the referee, Eugene Corri, felt moved to write:

"I had been prepared for something good from Basham, but not quite so good as we got. In attack and in defence he was brilliant, and to the expert lover of the game his display was a sheer delight. He could never afford to take things at all easily, and yet he always appeared to be boxing with genuine confidence. Wells tried his very hardest to get close to his opponent and hammer away at the body, but the splendidly effective cover-up of Basham was a perpetual stumbling block in his way. There was no suggestion of the American cover in Basham's methods — it was just most admirable defensive boxing.

His left leads were as good in their way as anything I have seen; timing and judgement of distance were alike consistently excellent. There may not have been a great deal of sting behind the glove, but it was impressively clever boxing.

Another phase of Basham's boxing that I admired very much was his ringcraft and generalship. He has not had a particularly long or varied experience of the game, but apparently he has little to learn in head-work. More than once he was in really tight corners, but always he was extremely sure of himself and never in the slightest degree flustered or

Matt Wells fought Johnny at the London Opera House.

haphazard. It was as well for him that he was not, for Wells was a most worrying and persistent opponent who was always working for a chance to send along a decisive punch."

As they clambered into the ring, the men provided a complete contrast in appearance. Basham was a "clean-limbed young fellow, lithe and graceful in all his movements" with the poise and balance of a "symmetrically proportional athlete." Matt Wells, on the other hand, was short and squat with a "real fighting face." With his "barrel of a chest" and well developed neck and shoulders, he made a formidable foe. Wells's main problem was his lack of height. He was a genuinely good boxer, but suffered from his lack of inches so that he had to get in close to make his punches count.

Matt Wells began the fight as a 7 to 4 on favourite and his tactics were clear from the start. He meant to rush Johnny at every available opportunity and try to break through his defences. Time and time again he used his strength in an attempt to batter his way through to Basham, but as Eugene Corri noted:

"the soldier was never once in a condition of anything approaching distress. He got just in front on points and was apparently satisfied to keep there, eschewing anything in the least risky, and carefully avoiding boxing that was merely flashy and spectacular."

At times Johnny reminded Corri forcibly of Jim Driscoll:

"There was not, perhaps, the sense of quiet mastery that used to be conveyed by the Welsh wonder, but there was much else that called to mind the late champion feather weight of the world."

As the bell for the last round sounded, the two men went at each other at a terrific pace. The hall was filled with the tremendous noise and din of the spectators, mainly soldiers in khaki uniforms, wildly cheering on their particular favourite. Many of those present thought that Wells had done just enough to earn a draw, others, in particular his own supporters, thought that he deserved to win, saying "that he had been knocking on the door" throughout the fight and should be declared the winner.

Unfortunately for them, the man whose job it was to make the decision thought otherwise. As Eugene Corri wrote later:

"Certainly to the uninitiated it may have looked as if Wells had been doing most of the work, but I had to remember that the door upon which he had so persistently been knocking had never opened. Basham had had his foot tight against it all the while, except when he opened it an inch or two to hit the man outside." The referee left the London Opera House

that night *"wondering where there was a better welterweight than this Welsh sergeant."*

The next day Johnny met Wells again when the stakes were being paid out. Wells's backer wanted a return, this time over twenty rounds, but Johnny just smiled and said "Your turn will come, Matt, and I'll always be glad to box such a good sport, but my next engagement is all fixed up." Wells stared at Johnny in surprise. "Who is your next opponent?" he asked. "Kaiser Bill" said Basham and continued pulling on his cigarette.

But before Johnny could get a crack at the Kaiser, he was the unwitting cause of another man being sent to France to face the German guns. That man was Robert Graves, poet, novelist and Royal Welch Fusilier. The author of, amongst other books, "Goodbye To All That" and "I, Claudius," Graves was desperate to join his brother officers in France, but still he languished in the depot at Wrexham, his Commanding Officer being reluctant to send him to the front as, somehow or other, he had earned himself a reputation for "unsportsmanlike behaviour." Graves had learned to box at Charterhouse public school and this, coupled with a chance encounter with Johnny Basham, would enable him to change his c.o's mind and be transferred to France. Ten years after the end of the war, Robert Graves recalled what happened in his autobiography, "Goodbye To All That."

"One by one my contemporaries were sent out to France to take the place of casualties in the first and second batallions, while I remained despondently at the depot. But again boxing helped me. Johnny Basham, a sergeant in the regiment, was training at the time for his fight — which he won — with Boswell (sic — Johnny never fought anyone of this name — Eddie Beattie, perhaps?) for the Lonsdale Belt, welterweight. I visited the training camp one evening, where Basham was offering to fight three rounds with any member of the regiment — the more the merrier. A young officer pulled on the gloves, and Basham got roars of laughter from the crowd as soon as he had taken his opponent's measure, by dodging around and playing the fool with him. I asked Basham's manager if I could have a go. He lent me some shorts, and I stepped into the ring. Pretending to know nothing of boxing, I led off with my right and moved clumsily. Basham saw a chance of getting another laugh; he dropped his guard and danced about with a you-can't-hit-me challenge. I caught him off his balance, and knocked him across the ring. He recovered and went for me, but I managed to keep on my feet. When I laughed at him, he laughed too. We had three very brisk rounds, and he very decently made

me seem a much better boxer than I was, by accommodating his pace to mine. As soon as Crawshay heard the story, he rang me up at my billet and told me that he had learned with pleasure of my performance; that for an officer to box like that was a great encouragement for the men; that he was mistaken about my sportsmanship; and that, to show his appreciation, he would put me down for a draft to France in a week's time."

As things turned out, Graves found himself transferred to a nightmare world where poison gas and German shell attacks were the norm and soldiers were sometimes sent "over the top" and to their deaths simply to "provide a diversion." In the end he could hardly face the men under his command and, to calm his shattered nerves, he began to drink about a bottle of whisky a day just to keep himself alive and awake.

Johnny was luckier. He was himself eventually transferred to France but not to the trenches and the front line. His first destination was St. Pol, where the Gymnastic staff under Colonel Campbell had its headquarters, and it was there that he renewed acquaintanceship with an old friend — "Peerless" Jim Driscoll:

"There were many other well-known boxers there. It was our job to show the boys the right way to do the physical jerks (how they blessed us) and time and time again we would make long journeys in the night in order to box an exhibition for some of the boys who had been wounded, and who preferred seeing Jim and I do our stuff to taking the "number nines" that the Medical Officer used to hand out! At this gymnastic job I had a fair run round, Amiens, Arras, Albert, Poperinghe, etc., etc., were all visited by Jim and I."

Driscoll and Basham were often used as "trouble-shooters" by Colonel Campbell during their time in France. Whenever there were difficulties between men just out of the front line and the military police, the cry went up, "Send for Driscoll and Basham," as it was said that the men would listen to them more "than they would take notice of a hundred Red Caps."

The two Welshmen usually managed to talk the hotheads round with a judicious mixture of conversation, tales about the old, pre-war days and blow by blow descriptions of their fights. They found that their Sergeants' stripes did not have the same "red rag to a bull" effect that those of other would-be peace makers might have had.

Once the two were sent on a mission and got rather more than they bargained for:

"The place we went to was well inside Jerry's gunfire, and I should have thought the boys would have been busy enough looking for a "Better

Ole" than fighting with nasty old Red Caps; but, there you are; a fellow must have his fun!

"Anyhow, here is the joke. When we arrived, the bother had been settled and the boys and the Red Caps were doing the lion and the lamb act, so Jim and I drank everybody's health and were thinking that life wasn't so bad when wheeee! a screech and a shell dropped close to the place where we were sitting.

"Now a big thing in this life is: Never look for trouble half-way. As soon as the shell hit the town I pointed out to my fellow-peace emissary, James Driscoll of the Welsh Horse, that as our work was done, neither he nor Sergeant Johnny Basham were needed any longer. The NEXT shell might carry an unlucky number.

"Jim and I went into conference on the matter, said conference lasted ten seconds, and then we were making the dust fly upon our way back to report to our O.C. that the trouble with the boys was over !

"And here is where our joke comes in. Jim and I walked into the O.C. with faces as solemn as a Scot when he sees an income-tax paper!

"You sent us to the wrong place, sir." This from both Driscoll and myself at once.

"Wrong place — how's that?" said the O.C. "Well, it was the wrong place for us sir, 'cause the Germans were shelling it!

"It is a good job for the pair of us that our O.C. was who he was, or had he been one of the ram-rod-up-his back type, our levity might have cost us dearly. As it was, a smile broke out on his face, and then we explained in detail all our doings."

That was typical of Basham and Driscoll. Welshmen both, the one from Newport, the other from Cardiff, they were separated by an age difference of ten years, but they had so much in common that they nevertheless formed an irrepressible double act. Perhaps it was the Irish blood in both of them. They liked nothing better than to rag one another unmercifully and, when they were together, the sparks literally flew. Johnny once confided in the referee, Eugene Corri, how Driscoll had won his promotion:

"Someone told me that Driscoll was wounded. I ran back and found him lying on the ground. I picked him up and carried him until I fell exhausted. Then he staggered to his feet just as the others arrived. They thought he had carried me — and that's how he won promotion."

But it was not all fun and games being a Physical Training Instructor with the Army in France. In his fictionalised account of the life and times of Jim Driscoll — "Peerless Jim Driscoll" — published in 1984, Alexander Cordell has Jim tell of the difficulties. He and the other training instructors were expected to take on all-comers, irrespective of what size or weight they were. Many times the opponent would be twice the size of the instructor and, what was worse, would not know how to pull his punches. His main, sometimes his only aim, was to land the one big punch which would floor Driscoll or Basham and enable him to say for the rest of his life: "I knocked out Johnny Basham," or "I put Jim Driscoll down for the count."

Cordell tellingly pin-pointed the training instructors' dilemma in an imaginary conversation between Driscoll and Basham:

"I've boxed a hundred rounds a week: I met Johnny Basham in a cafe in Arras, before the German attack, and he reckoned he was doing more. And I can remember to this day what Johnny said:

"' So, what can you do? If you take on a lad to give him a lesson in boxing, you can't say: ' Don't hit me hard, son, you're bigger than me,' or ' This is only a sparring session, lad, so be a sport and pull your punches.' and you'd likely take on another six like him that day after he'd come out of the shower.'"

One sparring partner that Johnny definitely did pull his punches with was the Prince of Wales. The future Edward VIII, and later Duke of Windsor, was touring the troops in an effort to boost morale when he was persuaded to pull on the gloves for a few brief rounds with Johnny. His Royal Highness emerging unscathed from his ordeal, Johnny promptly offered him a cigarette, saying, "Have a Woodbine, Sir." Laughingly, the Prince accepted Johnny's offer.

Royal interludes notwithstanding, there was no doubt in the minds of many boxing experts that this constant sparring with untrained soldiers was having a damaging effect on Johnny's boxing prowess. "Corinthian," writing in the "Lloyds Daily News" on Monday, February 3rd, 1919 stated bluntly that the work done by professional boxers in training soldiers might mean that they had got used to pulling their punches. This, in turn, meant that, when they did return to serious ring work, they had lost much of their power and precision. It was "Corinthian's" view that, when he fought Eddie Shevlin, Johnny had done so much "skipping about the ring" because he was unsure of his punching power.

There is no doubt that the war did have a damaging effect on Johnny's prospects as a professional boxer. It probably stopped him from going to America and it played havoc with his schedules so that he had to box professionally as and when he could. The military authorities were, it is true, sympathetic to his needs, but in time of war, the army had

"The Famous Six"
Back row, left to right: Bombardier Billy Wells, Pat O'Keefe, Johnny Basham, Dick Smith.
Front row, left to right: Jimmy Wilde, Captain Bruce Logan, Jim Driscoll.

first call on his services.

So it was that, in the early days of the war, and before his posting to France, he formed part of an elite corps of Army Physical Training Instructors. Under the command of Captain Bruce Logan, they toured Great Britain ready to take on all comers, a kind of military "super boxing-booth." There were six of them and they soon became known as "The Famous Six." And no wonder — when the six men involved were Johnny Basham, Jim Driscoll, Jimmy "The Mighty Atom" Wilde, Bombardier Wells, Pat O'Keefe and Dick Smith. Eventually they went their different ways and Basham and Driscoll met up again in France.

One man who came across them there was Norman Clark, the author of "All In The Game." A keen boxer, Clark was more than pleased to find himself amongst such illustrious company:

"Outside the bout with Sergeant Jack Kelly, which I mentioned in the second chapter of this book, I did not get any proper boxing in France until I was sent to St. Pol on a G.H.Q. Physical Training and Bayonet Fighting Course. On leaving for this it never occurred to me that I was in for anything but one of the ordinary rather tedious courses, and I did not expect to see any one I knew; but no sooner had I arrived at St. Pol than I found first one old acquaintance and then another. The place seemed to be virtually run by various people I had previously met in the boxing world. In command was Colonel R. Campbell, who had judged me in the Public Schools Championships as far back as 1910; with him, as second in command, was Major W. Delaney, who, at the time when he used to act as M.C. at the Cosmopolitan Gymnasium, Plymouth, always came to judge our boxing and gymnastics at Blundell's School; and amongst the leading Sergeant-Major Instructors were such well-known boxers as Jim Driscoll, Johnny Basham, Billy Wells, and several others whom I knew. To me the chief attraction was, of course, Jim Driscoll, who had always been my beau ideal of a champion; and I was delighted to see him in such good trim; and to hear confirmed by him the rumour that he was shortly returning to the Ring. Unfortunately Driscoll had to go away a few days after I arrived; but there still remained Johnny Basham, who was then the best and cleverest exponent of the English style of boxing after Driscoll himself. During the three weeks I spent at St. Pol, Basham and I boxed together frequently, and I greatly enjoyed and profited by the experience. In addition to being a great boxer, he was a real good fellow was Basham, full of fun and liveliness, and yet withal gentle-natured, and when he used to come and have supper with me at my billet (about the only decent house I ever stayed at in France) we thoroughly enjoyed ourselves. At that

Norman Clark sparring with Johnny.

time he was right in his prime, and no one in England at his weight had a look in with him."

Despite his duties as both boxing instructor and "trouble-shooter," Johnny did occasionally get leave and it was then that he was able, once more, to pick up the threads of his boxing career. On one such visit to Britain he fought Sid Burns at Holborn on May 28th, 1917. It was a bout which very nearly proved to be a date with disaster for Basham. Jack Goodwin, Burns's trainer, recalled the contest in his book, "Myself and My Boxers,"

"On his (Sid Burns's) return to England he was called to the Colours, and once he had settled down to Army life he began to give his mind to boxing again.

"One day when I was at the Holborn Stadium. Mr. Jack Callaghan told me he was looking for an opponent for Johnny Basham.

"' Why not Sid Burns?' I suggested. ' He would make a real good match with Basham.'

"Callaghan approved of the idea, so I wrote to Burns, who at the time was doing special work in the motor transport at Osterley Park.

"Burns was delighted with the prospect of a real fight, and the match was made, but he was unable to get leave for proper training. He wrote me that he was going to do his utmost to win and, if not in fighting trim, he was at least in excellent health.

"I was able to get Burns to come to Whetstone on the Saturday before the contest, where he did an hour's gymnasium work and I massaged him thoroughly. Then he had to get back to barracks and I did not see him again till the Monday evening at Holborn Stadium

"One hour's preparation for a battle with a top-notcher like Johnny Basham was perilously little, for Burns was not a Harry Stone, and I knew he would have to win quickly as he would never last twenty hard rounds.

"Though I sent him out for the first round with definite instructions, Sid was too good a boxer to take a risk with the famous Welshman. For quite a while they sparred for an opening.

"Then, suddenly, out shot Burns's right hand, catching Basham on the point of the jaw. Down went the welter-weight champion as if he had been pole-axed, and nearly everyone thought the fight was all over. They had not counted on Basham's amazing pluck and endurance. He was up at the count of nine, and with that wonderful cleverness that has made him such an idol of the Ring, he managed to last out the round without getting hit again.

Johnny!

"I could see that Basham was very dazed when he came up for the second round, and Burns went out to fight like a tiger. Once he caught Johnny on the mouth and cut the inside of his lip badly, but he could not again get past that invulnerable guard.

"Basham that night fought as clever a battle as he did later in his first contest with Kid Lewis, and gradually he began to shake off the effects of that terrible knock-down punch.

"After the eighth round Sid Burns came back to his corner very distressed; not from punishment, but lack of condition. It was just what I had feared.

"'Jack,' he said, 'I wish I had been well for this contest. I feel licked now.'

"'Never mind, just do your best,' I consoled. But as I bent down to get the sponge from the pail one of his other seconds who was using the towel, hearing Sid's remark, flung it into the ring. That, of course, put an end to the fight, but I should certainly have let my man chance his arm for another round or two, for he had not been badly punished."

CHAPTER VIII
The Last Hurrah

*"And Those Last Rounds?
Don't Ask Me To Remember
Them, They Were Just One
Whirl Of Blows."*

At the end of the war Johnny returned to Wrexham where, once again, his talents as a "trouble shooter" were in great demand. Drunkenness amongst the troops had greatly increased under the kind hearted but ineffectual rule of one commanding officer. This all changed when he was replaced by a regular "fire-eater" who soon found the answer to the drink problem.

"Drunk?" he would say to the man standing in front of him. "Yes, sir", came the reply. "Right, into the gym with Johnny Basham for three minutes." Needless to say, as the word got round, there was a sharp fall in the rate of drunkenness. At the same time the Regimental Police patrolled the town with Johnny Basham, who would cross the road, deal with a drunken man and the patrol would take him away.

But it was not long before Johnny was after bigger fish than the "drunk and disorderlys" from the ranks of the R.W.F. Between January 1919 and April 1920 he fought nine times, never losing and drawing only once. It was to be his last great flourish. He began by meeting George "Kid" Plested of Birmingham over twenty three-minute-rounds at the Liverpool Stadium. The "Kid" was a rising star who for some time had carried all before him in the welterweight division, and his heavy punching had proved too much for his previous opponents. Against Basham, however, Plested was a huge disappointment. He went down in the eighth after a heavy body punch and, in the twelfth, was disqualified for holding.

Johnny now moved down to London and the National Sporting Club where Eddie Shevlin, welterweight champion of the American navy, was ready to face him for a side wager and the club purse of £550. A Chief Petty Officer, Shevlin was a native of Boston. At the weigh-in, Basham had the advantage of a few inches in height and he was also a half-pound heavier. The opening bell sounded on January 27th, 1919 and Johnny set off at a tremendous pace, threatening to completely

The cartoonist Tom Webster gives his view of the Basham v Shevlin fight.

overwhelm the American. But Shevlin stuck to his task and refused to go under, despite the hail of blows coming at him from all directions, and he was still standing at the end of the contest, despite being a clear loser on points.

After the fight, the "Daily Telegraph" reflected that Johnny "was always pretty to watch but now and then he used up his energy quite unnecessarily. He was given to sacrificing sheer fighting for the spectacular." In the "Daily Mail," "Berkeley" considered that £450 was not bad for fifteen rounds work and continued:

"What place in the category of great British boxers shall we allot to Johnny Basham, the welterweight champion of England? My personal view is that his position ought to be an exalted one. On the display he gave against Eddie Shevlin, the welterweight champion of the United States Navy, at the National Sporting Club on Monday evening, Basham is fully entitled to be rated as one of the most accomplished boxers that ever put up a hand. He has style, variety and speed in great abundance, his footwork is remarkably clever, and he uses his brains all the time he is in the ring."

Describing Shevlin as a "very tough, clever customer," "Berkeley" quoted one member of the NSC's Committee as saying, "Well, you have seen Shevlin beaten by the only man in England capable of defeating him." *"High praise,"* wrote "Berkeley," *"but by no means too high. Besides boxing cleverly the American boxed cleanly, and in the most sportsmanlike way. Once he hit Basham a little low, but he expressed his regret at once and his following work was characterised by extreme carefulness."* "Berkeley" concluded his tribute to Basham by saying:

"If Monday's victor has a fault, it is that he throws himself open with surprising frequency and apparent carelessness. He has also a fondness for leading with the right, which may one day prove costly to him. But Basham's footwork is so remarkably good, and his speed so intense, that he can, perhaps, afford to take risks which would be a positive danger to one not so plentifully endowed with these qualities. There is a deal in the method of Jimmy Wilde about Basham: indeed, when he is "mixing it" he reminds one forcefully of the little "Welsh wonder." What a trinity Driscoll, Wilde and Basham make to be sure — for I am informed that they are all as Welsh as Mr. Lloyd George himself. Wales has every reason to be proud of these three."

But Eddie Shevlin and his friends were not convinced. They took heart at the American's good showing over fifteen rounds and reasoned that Basham would not be able to maintain his remarkable pace over the longer distance of twenty rounds. Basham was willing to give him his chance but first he had a date with Kid Doyle at the Liverpool Stadium. It was February 22nd, and Johnny's fellow Welshman from Llwynypia in the Rhondda, had a surprise in store for the "Happy Warrior." In round two, after a "rough rally," Doyle unceremoniously crashed Johnny to the boards with a right hook to the jaw. Basham soon got to his feet, but his face began to wear "a very anxious expression." Now he knew he was in a fight. Slowly, he began to claw his way back. Doyle was still dangerous but, by the end of the twenty rounds, Johnny had done just enough to snatch the decision on points.

The close call against Kid Doyle must have given Eddie Shevlin fresh heart when he encountered the Lonsdale Belt holder for the second time at the NSC on St. Patrick's Night, March 17th, 1919. "Good Boy, Eddie," shouted the American's supporters as he attempted to win the lion's share of the £100 each man had put up and the NSC purse of £500. He failed. Basham outpointed him once again but he could not drop the tough Irish American. Johnny peppered his opponent's jaw with shots that would have floored many a lesser man, but Shevlin only shook his head and came right on coming. As the "Empire News" said, Eddie must have had a jaw like cast iron, and he was certainly durable, but according to "Sportsman" he was outclassed from start to finish. He had plenty of pluck and stamina, but he was simply not in it with Johnny Basham as a points scorer.

Other critics were less impressed by Johnny's performance. One who represented the "purist" viewpoint was "Berkeley" of the "Daily Mail." He told his readers:

"No one can convince me there is any justification for Basham leading with the right as he did on Monday. Only in the case of a man of Basham's remarkable speed can there be any excuse for the use of the right as Basham used it on Monday evening. Had Shevlin been as fast as Basham he would have chopped off his head with his left, even though that was not a very straight weapon.

"Basham and his friends may not think so, but his fondness for the right lead is spoiling his otherwise very fine left. Basham's judgement of distance with the left is not by any means what it was. He missed frequently with the left on Monday and exhibited a lack of direction with the left which is not usual with him. He gives me the impression that if he persists in his present methods he won't last long against someone as fast as he is — one who has a moderately good left and knows how to use it."

But "Berkeley" did sweeten the "pill" to some extent by further

The quality of this old photograph, taken outside the Nag's Head, Wrexham, in 1919, leaves something to be desired, but it is still of interest. Sitting on Johnny's knee is James Edwards, the son of Walter Edwards, Johnny's trainer. Also in the group are Bill Mortimer, Johnny's backer, Walter Edwards, his trainer, and, in the second row, on Johnny's right, Fred Rowland.

informing his readers that:

"Johnny Basham has a combination of abilities and defects that renders him one of the most interesting boxing personalities of the last twenty years. For a man who has to earn his living by the giving and taking of "plaguey knocks" he has a strange yet admirable temperament. I don't believe he could be vicious or bear malice towards an opponent if he tried. Serious and in deadly earnest, yes, but never blood-thirsty, as so many so-called patrons of the sport seem desperately anxious that every boxer should be."

Another American, Augie Ratner, was the next man to fancy his chances against Johnny Basham. A former amateur champion of the United States, he stepped into the ring at the NSC for what were to prove twenty long, hard and testing rounds for a stake and purse aggregating £1,200. As usual, Johnny had trained at Wrexham and knew that he would be up against a tough and difficult opponent, but he still felt confident:

"I never felt in finer condition, and I certainly hope to win, although admitting that I shall be conceding a lot of weight to a first-class American who will probably be a stone heavier when we enter the ring. If condition counts for anything, then I have a great chance."

In years to come, Johnny Basham was to look back on his struggle with Ratner as one of his finest ever contests, especially as he was giving away weight to his opponent. Ratner was widely regarded as an experienced and crafty boxer, who would give Basham a run for his money, and so it proved. The American began the fight well and looked to be more than justifying the odds laid on him before the bout began, but then Johnny started to catch up. His speed started to make itself felt and, very soon, the betting began to swing in his favour. Left jab after elegant left jab piled up the points for the Welshman and, by the fifteenth, he appeared to be well on the way to victory but:

"When the fifteenth round came along those behind the American must have told him he was behind on points, for he came after me like an express train run amok! And those last rounds? Don't ask me to remember them, they were just one whirl of blows, and we were smashing away at each other when the final bell rang."

Most people thought Johnny had done enough to clinch the win, but the referee, Mr. Douglas, clearly thought otherwise as he had both men level on points at the end. The Ratner fight out of the way, Johnny scarcely paused for breath in his breakneck search for fresh opponents. This time it was Willie Farrell, of Southwark, who had made a name for

Pen Pictures of the Boxers.

JOHNNY BASHAM

The Jimmy Wilde of the Welter division. Is a human motorcar of the speediest make. Unpuncturable over twenty rounds. Can travel top speed over any gradient. Has been well brought up. His legs have been taught that his face is sacrosant. Though not exactly an Adonis he loves his face too well to have it knocked about. Victory means a match with Jack Britton, of America. The latter recently outpointed Mike O'Dowd. Also beat Ted Kid Lewis. Basham and the proletariat are strangers—almost. He has seldom fought outside the Club. Will he win? All Wales says "Yes!"

FRANCIS CHARLES

Is French to the finger-tips. Wears the Croix de Guerre and another distinction for valour in the field. Fought in the Dardanelles and escaped without a scratch. Is tough and game as befits a medallist. Will need to be both as his science is not comparable to Basham's. Is a fighter rather than a boxer. In the matter of weight is a trifle lighter than his opponent. Am told that Basham will never knock him out. The Asquithian dictum seems applicable here—"Wait and see."

The French Champion Francis Charles.

himself by recently disposing of the three "Kids" — Messrs. Plested, Doyle and Carter. The fight took place at the Pudsey-Street stadium in Liverpool and it would be the last time that Johnny would fight on his old "stomping ground." The fight was scheduled for the full twenty rounds, but never got that far, as Johnny left his Liverpool supporters with something to remember him by, Willy Farrell being forced to retire in the eleventh round.

Attempts were now made to get Johnny into the same ring as Francis Charles, the French war hero and holder of the *Croix de Guerre.* By 1928, Charles would be blind and helpless, but now, in 1919, he was the welterweight champion of all France. He met Johnny Basham at the London Olympia on September 2nd, in a fight billed by some as being for the European Welterweight title. The Frenchman started off at an amazing pace and threatened to sweep Basham away altogether. Johnny had great difficulty in stopping Charles's impetuous onrushes, but by the end of the round, he was beginning to exert his customary ring presence; the left hand was starting to work and Charles was slowing down.

The rather flowery programme notes for the night referred to Johnny as:

"The Jimmy Wilde of the Welter division. Is a human motorcar of the speediest make. Unpuncturable over twenty rounds. Can travel top speed over any gradient. Has been well brought up. His legs have been taught that his face is sacrosanct. Though not exactly an Adonis he loves his face too well to have it knocked about."

What exactly the "human motorcar" thought about all this has never been recorded, but he certainly turned on the style against the Frenchman, despite going down for a count of "seven" in the seventh round. Charles could not maintain the madcap pace of the first few rounds and Basham won easily enough on points over the full distance.

Johnny now faced Matt Wells for the third time at the Holborn Stadium on November 13th, 1919. At stake were Johnny's British title and the Empire title belonging to Wells. It was a hard, bruising contest, so much so that "Berkeley" of the "Daily Mail" felt duty-bound to write:

"Johnny Basham is the most ill-used boxer of our time. He is always running up against opponents whose proportion of skill is not quite equal to his own... His latest experience with Matt Wells must, I am afraid, be accounted his worst... he had to suffer usage from which the referee ought to have protected him but did not. In face of the provocation to which Basham had to submit the ordinary person may have been surprised that he did not give tit for tat but these people do not know Johnny Basham,

Matt Wells versus Johnny Basham as seen by Tom Webster of the "Evening News".

the lad has the most delicate feelings in regard to what he believes to be the unwritten laws of the sport, and I know that he would rather lose a contest than transgress any of them. For that reason the fighting style of Wells was most exasperating, to say the least — Basham's forehead was cut in two places — once by a distinct scrub of the head — Basham is not a perfect boxer — there isn't such a thing — but he is certainly a stylist of a very high order. And he is flawless in regard to fairness of method. He would have been grieved had he won by the disqualification of his opponent on Thursday night, and yet, if ever a man had cause for complaint, he had."

And indeed he had. When "Berkeley" went to see Johnny on the day after the fight, he found that the champion's left collar bone was so raw that he had to have a pad of cooling ointment on it. After this bruising encounter, Johnny waited another five months before his next ring match. This time the chosen opponent was Fred Kay, an Australian southpaw, who had disposed of some formidable American opposition. The contest, held over twenty rounds, was billed as being for the Welterweight Championship of the British Empire. The venue was the National Sporting Club, the purse was for £1,400 and the date was April 12th, 1920.

Kay was five foot ten and a half inches, but what puzzled Basham most was his unorthodox, right foot forward stance — as never before had Johnny encountered a "southpaw." Twice the Welshman adopted his opponent's style, but he soon abandoned it, and went back to his usual method of fighting. Kay had a reputation for speed — he was said to be able to go backwards faster than most men could go forwards — but he showed little evidence of this against Johnny; it being the Newport man who continually forced the pace. Indeed, Basham proved to be much more skilful than Kay, but he had difficulty in landing his punches effectively against Kay's awkward style. The Australian never once used his left, being content merely to poke out his right, but Johnny knew too much for him. After the halfway mark, he dominated the contest, and it was only Kay's long reach and awkward stance that saved him from utter humiliation. As it was, Johnny won round after round and was well ahead on points by the end of the contest.

Before the fight there had been many ready to back Kay, because of his previous record, but they were to be sadly disappointed. Johnny himself never had any doubts, as the "Old Guard" later disclosed to his readers:

"Our champion was very confident before-hand. I met him at half past seven wandering down the Strand instead of taking the rest most

Southpaw Fred Kay gave Johnny a few problems at first.

boxers indulge in before a fight. Later — at ten o' clock to be exact —I again encountered him leaving the Club. These acts would be attributed to nervousness if performed by some boxers, but Basham is far too seasoned a boxer to be accused of nervousness."

The Kay fight was Johnny's last appearance at the National Sporting Club, he had fought there eight times in all. Many of the club's members were convinced he was the premier welterweight in Britain, if not the world, and would certainly have agreed with "Corinthian's" assessment, made in the "Sporting Chronicle," a year before the Kay fight:

"No boxer deserves to be a world champion more than the brainy Welshman. He has all the exuberance of a happy schoolboy, and revels in joke; yet in action he is a perfect machine. His determination and strategy are of the highest calibre and like a professional billiards player he is always looking ahead. Sometimes he misses a lead purposely and it is obvious he intends coaxing his man into a vulnerable position."

Following his defeat of Fred Kay, Johnny had reached his peak. He was now British, European and Empire Welterweight Champion. Only the world title eluded him. His position seemed secure — yet the "happy schoolboy" was soon to face his severest test. Would he be equal to the challenge?

CHAPTER IX

Waiting for Lewis

"No! No! I Have Not Given In, Let Me Go On."

No champion, however good, lasts forever, there is always a new challenger waiting in the wings, ready and willing to relieve the champion of his title. Sooner or later, the champion must fall, unless, of course, he retires undefeated. But the champion who retires undefeated is rare indeed. Such thoughts were far from Johnny Basham's mind at the beginning of 1920. He had survived the war in one piece, unlike many of his boxing contemporaries, he was undisputed champion of Great Britain and there appeared to be little threat to his position from British based boxers. He could afford to be well pleased with himself. But there was a cloud on Johnny's near perfect horizon and it was growing bigger with each passing day.

That cloud went by the name of Gershon Mendeloff. Scarcely a name to put fear and dread into the hearts of the timid, but there was another name by which Gershon Mendeloff was better known. That name was Ted "Kid" Lewis and that was a name to conjure with. Mendeloff/Lewis had landed in Southampton on Tuesday, November 18th, 1919 having crossed the Atlantic on board the White Star Liner, Laplands. Born in Aldgate in the East End of London, Lewis was the son of a Jewish cabinet maker from the East End of London.

For his first fight, Lewis received sixpence and a cup of coffee. Before he was twenty he had succeeded Jim Driscoll as British Featherweight champion by beating Alec Lambert at the NSC in 1913. This brought him a coveted Lonsdale Belt but, after leaving for America, he began to put on weight and had to return it.

In the States he was looked upon as something of a freak because of his ability to fight one week as a featherweight, the next as a lightweight, and the week after that as a welter. To increase the air of mystery surrounding his fighter, Lewis's trainer let it be known that he supplied Ted with a mysterious draught which allowed him to meet whatever fighting weight he needed. Something of an innovator, the Kid once had his right hand insured for the sum of £3,000.

Whilst in America Lewis featured in a titanic series of struggles with

Ted "Kid" Lewis — the one man Johnny could never beat.

Jack Britton for the world welterweight title. Britton, an Irish American from Clinton, Iowa, actually fought Lewis no less than an amazing twenty times, the fights taking place in as many as twelve different American cities. On one memorable occasion, in June 1917, they actually fought each other three times in the space of nineteen days.

There was little, therefore, anyone could teach Ted Lewis about boxing and when, after an absence of five years, he landed in Britain, he wasted no time in cutting a swathe through the ranks of British boxers. They went down before him like tin soldiers in the path of a Sherman tank.

On Boxing Day, 1919 he stopped Matt Wells at the Albert Hall. On Friday, March 5th, 1920 he hammered Gus Platts into submission before a vast crowd in Sheffield, Platts's seconds throwing in the towel in the eighteenth round. Six days later he knocked out Birkenhead's Johnny Bee in the fourth round. On Monday, April 5th he beat Kid Doyle at the Liverpool Stadium. This time the towel was thrown into the ring in the eleventh round.

Doyle was not convinced and needed to be defeated again at London's Holborn Stadium on Friday, April 30th. The towel fluttered across the ring in round five. Frank Moody at Manchester and Jerry Shea at Mountain Ash gave the "Kid" and the referee little trouble, each of them going in round one.

So, step by step, Lewis was coming closer to Basham. Like a medieval knight in armour in some ancient tale of chivalry, he was gradually sweeping away all the obstacles that lay between him and the object of his quest, the champion. Basham was the "King of the Castle" and Lewis intended to dethrone him. The Championship, that "Holy Grail" of British boxing belonged to Basham and Lewis intended to deprive him of it.

If the Basham camp felt any alarm at this latest threat to their man's well-being, they did not show it. Indeed, there had already been much speculation in the British Press about a possible match between Johnny and Lewis for the Welterweight Championship of the world. The NSC had put up a purse of £2,000 and intended holding the contest on Derby night.

All bets were off, however, once Lewis lost his title to Jack Britton in nine rounds. Lewis's manager claimed that he was sick but, as he did not want to disappoint the fans, he fought Jack Britton. It was only weakness that caused him to fall in the sixth and seventh, finally collapsing in the ninth. There was also confusion as to whether the fight had actually been for the world championship. Some reports stated that the two men had fought at catchweights, and at a shorter distance than the championship course, in which case Lewis would have retained his title.

Unimpressed, the "Sporting Chronicle" muttered darkly that, if only Lewis had stuck to his original plan of returning to England once the danger of air-raids and war service had passed, he would probably have been fighting Basham at the NSC for the World Championship.

Just before the Basham-Eddie Shevlin fight, William Mortimer, Basham's backer, told "Corinthian" of the "Sporting Chronicle" that, in the event of a Basham v. Lewis fight, Basham would have to be guaranteed the lion's share of the purse. He was, after all, the undisputed Welterweight champion of Great Britain and had yet to lose a fight in London. Mortimer further hinted that Johnny's next move might be to move up to the middle-weight class.

Then Mortimer wrote to the "Sporting Chronicle", saying that *"after Kid Lewis's latest showing, sick or well, we do not want him, but I will match Johnny Basham with his conqueror — Jack Britton — for the best purse offered, and I will have a fair-sized stake on the result. The best is good enough for Basham and also for the British boxing public. That match — Basham and Britton — would, indeed, be a fine drawing card, for Britton was an American before the war, and, to my mind, he is the man entitled to box a Britisher for the title of Welterweight Champion of the world. If you cannot get him over here, I shall take Basham over to America, if only for the one contest; that is, when he can get his discharge out of the army."*

The newspaper war of words continued when Lewis's brother-in-law, M.E. Lyttleston, wrote to the "Sporting Life," complaining that people seemed to think Lewis had deliberately run away from England to dodge the army when, in actual fact, he had left nearly five months before the war started and was in Australia.

He then moved on to America but the British Army there rejected him because of hammered toes and flat feet. Lyttleston claimed he had proof of this. Instead of coming to England to get a nice cushy staff job, Lewis had joined the U.S. army as a boxing instructor.

On Monday, April 19th, 1920 representatives of Basham and Lewis met at Hammersmith where articles were signed and a sum of £2,000 deposited as a guarantee. The match was to be for £5,000, one of the highest priced fights ever to be staged in Great Britain, of which the winner would take sixty per cent, with the rest falling to the loser. (£5,000 does not sound very much by today's prices, but in the 1920s it was a considerable amount of money. Indeed, it would have been worth more than a £15,000 purse offered to Brian Curvis for his World Welter-weight title fight with Emile Griffith in 1964. So that, as far as Basham and Lewis were concerned, it was a fortune worth fighting for.) On May 3rd, 1920, it was announced that the fight would take place at the Olympia in London on June 9th.

Now the experts began to wonder whether Johnny would be able to stand up to the pounding Lewis was sure to give him. Would he be able to get enough strength behind his immaculate straight left to fend off the Aldgate "Juggernaut" when he rushed him, as he was sure to do?

The "Old Guard" lamented the fact that before Lewis left Britain he was both a boxer and a fighter. "Now he relies almost solely on fighting — and very rugged stuff at that." According to the "Old Guard," "Lewis's abnormal strength comes from his build. Above the thighs he is built like a heavy-weight."

In the "Old Guard's" opinion Lewis was going to beat Basham, but many unbiased judges thought the opposite, and based their assessment upon Basham's speed preventing Lewis from getting in close, where he was so deadly.

The "Wrexham Advertiser's" reporter visited Johnny's training quarters to see how he was preparing for this all important fight with Lewis. Johnny's trainer, Walter Edwards, organised his routine which started at eight o'clock in the morning. Basham would run and walk alternately for ten to thirteen miles around the lanes surrounding Wrexham, shadow boxing all the while en route. On return to base he took a bath and was then free until six in the evening when he began his more strenuous gym and ring work.

When the reporter arrived at the Barracks gymnasium, Johnny was already hard at work, skipping backwards and forwards. He then took to ball-punching and other in-between exercises before the arrival of his four sparring partners. Without pausing for breath, Johnny immediately launched into a series of eighteen three-minute rounds with the four men, giving a display of his skills which was greatly appreciated by the watching public.

Johnny was under no illusions as to the difficulties of the task awaiting him — reports from Lewis's training camp on the South Coast at Brighton had him very fit and well — but, his training over, he had this to say to the local reporter:

"I am in fit trim, and well, and all I can say is that I hope the best boy will win. I go down to London with every hope, and I have no complaints

to make."

Johnny's trainer also had high hopes:

"I have been with him to nearly all his chief fights, and my opinion is that I have never seen him better than he is now. He is as fit as a fiddle, and I hope to see him win. He is as fit now as he ever was in his life, and you can rest assured that when the time comes he will be ready to fight for his life."

Walter Edwards went on to say that Johnny was *"always willing and ready to do anything. After his morning run, he returns as fresh as when he started, and following a few exercises and having his muscles massaged he sets down comfortably for the remainder of his day until time for the gym at night."*

Johnny was already down to the weight, with a good allowance for travelling. He planned to finish his training on the Monday, and leave for London on the Tuesday afternoon in good time for the weigh-in on Wednesday, at 2 o'clock. His seconds were expected to be Walter Edwards, Mr. Hanmer of Chester and two others chosen by the promoters.

On the day of the fight, the "Daily Express" plumped for Lewis, citing his advantage in years, and his riper and more varied experience with boxers of a much higher class than Basham had been used to. In the "Daily News," Fred Dartnell referred to Johnny's habit of starting slowly and reflected that he might be caught in the first few rounds — Basham was undeniably a class fighter but he lacked "Kid" Lewis's punch.

Right from the start of the fight, Lewis, who was clearly anxious to establish his superiority, rushed at Johnny. Most of these fierce assaults Johnny managed to beat off with some superb left hand work, but enough of them succeeded to get the Lewis fans in the audience whooping with delight. Johnny refused to panic and treated the crowd to a demonstration of his boxing skills. As long as he could keep the fight at long range, he was in with a chance. It was at close quarters that Lewis's powerful upper-cuts and jabs were capable of wreaking terrible damage.

In round three the incident occurred which changed the whole course of the fight. Johnny was not wearing a gumshield and one of Lewis's blows forced a tooth through his lower lip. Blood poured from the wound and Johnny was obviously in desperate trouble. Still refusing to panic, the champion immediately switched to the defensive tactics of which he was such a master.

At the end of round three Johnny's chief second, Danny Davies, and the rest of his corner men worked furiously to repair the damage. The

In his eagerness to get at Johnny, the "Kid" almost stumbles.

ringside doctor was all for stopping the fight at once, but as Johnny still felt strong and confident, the Basham camp would not hear of this.

In round four a cut opened above Johnny's eye and Lewis ruthlessly began to target almost all his blows on to that cut. In the sixth Johnny boxed well but he still returned to his corner with blood flowing freely from a cut on the mouth. Now Lewis concentrated all his attacks on one or the other of Johnny's cuts. There was nothing personal about it, that was just the way he operated — "he asked for no quarter and so gave none."

By the beginning of the seventh round, Johnny's manager, Will Dodman, had added his voice to that of Danny Davies, and pleaded with Johnny to "turn it in," telling him they would get Ted again, but Johnny was stubborn and insisted on continuing.

In the eighth round Johnny showed "most gallant boxing." Knowing that he was weakening and the end might soon be near, he tried his best to finish the fight. As always, his chosen weapon was the left. In and out it darted, beating out a rhythm of such strength and forcefulness on Lewis's face that the Londoner was astonished.

Nevertheless, the Welshman was still very shaken at the end of the eighth round. He was now very weak from loss of blood and, seeing his plight, his chief second threw in the towel. As it floated into the ring, Johnny leapt from his seat and, his eyes brimming with tears, implored the referee to continue the fight. "No! No! I have not given in, let me go on," he cried. As he did so, his seconds dragged him "struggling and protesting" back to his corner, leaving the referee with little choice but to give the fight to Ted "Kid" Lewis.

It was revealed after the fight that it was an old tooth that had been driven into Johnny's lower lip. He had to have surgical attention at Charing Cross Hospital and three stitches were put in.

Meanwhile, as the fight was going on, the people of North Wales waited. Hundreds of them lined the streets of Wrexham waiting for news from the Olympia. As they waited, they whiled away the time wondering whether Basham would stand up to the fierce batterings of Lewis over the full twenty rounds. The general opinion was that if Basham could only last the course, victory was sure to be his. Rumours were rife, yet the crowd hesitated to give vent to a cheer until the result was declared officially.

Around eleven o'clock, the news came through that Johnny had been forced to retire in the ninth and a disappointed crowd, still hopeful that there would be some satisfactory reason for this reverse, went home in an orderly manner.

In South Wales, in Johnny's home town of Newport, a crowd had gathered outside the High Street offices of the local newspaper, "The South Wales Argus," to hear the result — "The road was crowded with enthusiasts, and passing vehicles had a difficulty in getting through." But the result, when it came, was disappointing and the crowd dispersed much quicker than it had assembled and "without a murmur."

After the fight, the newspapers gave their verdicts. The "Times" thought that the end was unsatisfactory and left undecided the question as to who really was the better man of the two. In the "Sportsman," "L.S.D." reflected on what kind of a man it was that Johnny had so recently faced in the ring:

"His face is a mask, impenetrable. You cannot judge what his intentions are. He is brainy in the ring without a doubt, but ice-cold with it. He is remorseless. He feels certain that Basham cannot hurt him or; at least, that is how he impresses one. By the ardour of his close-in fighting he wishes to get a quick verdict, but if it does not succeed — and it did not — well, he is perfectly self possessed. He is built to stay; ready to wait and see. He has tried to unsettle, to unship Basham at the very outset, but his greater power of punch has not prevailed. He is calm, even philosophical; quite content to take what Basham can hand out, waiting, ever-waiting, for a chance to catch his rival in an unguarded moment, when the full damage may be done with tigerish ferocity..."

In the "Daily Chronicle," "Corinthian" wrote:

"As far as actual boxing ability went Basham defeated Lewis, and it is highly probable that, had he escaped that punctured lip, he would have received the verdict on points. Basham was wonderful in his pluck, but a boxer must have blood, and, although Basham lost so much by this unlucky injury, which caused blood to spurt from his lip like water from a tap, he was still boxing strongly when the contest was stopped at the end of the ninth."

Corinthian continued: *"Still the British champion boxed back with splendid courage and amazing skill. Lewis was flabbergasted by the pace of the punching that checked him, and to those who knew the effects of the loss of blood the pity was that so good a boxer should be so near to approaching defeat from a man whom he could beat."*

The "Daily Graphic" was not so charitable. Its reporter felt that *"Johnny Basham made the greatest mistake of his life when he imagined that he could beat Ted "Kid" Lewis at fighting. He had the better and the straighter left hand, but he was, as most feared he would be, lamentably short in punching power."*

"Berkeley" in the "Daily Mail" disagreed:

"This was a great contest, and although beaten Basham has never fought in better style. Against a much stronger man he showed that skill can prevail in all the finer points of the game."

Johnny himself, as always, put a brave face on events. Talking after the fight, he said:

"I had been told before-hand that Lewis was a tremendous hitter, and when I went to bed last night after duly celebrating my defeat I was prepared this morning to discover numerous bruises on my ribs. But there wasn't a sign of one, nor was there any soreness. I think I was unlucky to run into the punch which cut my lip so badly, as if I had evaded it, I feel sure I would have outpointed him."

Ted Kid Lewis praised his beaten opponent. Speaking in an interview after the fight he said, *"Basham is the greatest man I ever fought. He was as game as a whistle and gave me a tremendous fight."*

Lewis could afford to be generous. He had taken on and beaten the best that Britain had to offer and, finally, dethroned the reigning champion. But even as he said these words, plans were already being made for a Basham v. Lewis rematch. Johnny's camp was certain that he would never have lost if he had been wearing a gumshield.

As for Lewis, he was not against giving Johnny another chance. He himself had suffered in the past because of his own irregular teeth bleeding unnecessarily, and had taken the trouble to visit a dentist who had fitted him with a rubber mouth protector. Now the Kid offered to have one made for Johnny so that, the next time they met, it would be on more equal terms.

In the meantime, Johnny travelled home to Wrexham where he was given a hero's welcome. As his train pulled into the station around ten o'clock at night, there was a fair-sized crowd waiting on the platform including the Mayor. As the "Wrexham Advertiser" put it:

"The train being of considerable length, it was at first difficult to locate the carriage in which the boxer travelled. A shout of "Where are you, Johnny?" brought the response of "Here he is," from the latter end of the train, and instantly the crowd rushed forward, regardless of luggage which had been put out of the train, and Basham, who did not show much sign of the time he had gone through the previous night, was in a trice hoisted on the shoulders of his eager friends. At the foot of the bridge stairs, the Mayor addressed Basham and wrung his hand warmly, saying, 'We are proud to welcome you back home. We are proud of you and what

you have done. Although you have not been the victor, we feel the better man of the contest has come to Wrexham.'"

Johnny modestly thanked the Mayor and then, still shoulder high, he was carried over the bridge and down to the station exit where an even greater number of people awaited him. Indeed, so great was the crush that the waiting "motor car" could not be started and had to be pulled along the streets amidst scenes of "tumultuous excitement."

Every so often, a halt would be called and the Mayor would inform the waiting crowds that Johnny had arranged another fight with Kid Lewis and, what was more, he was ready to place a bet of one thousand pounds of his own money that he would soon be bringing back the belt to Wrexham.

At last, in the words of the "Advertiser," the Mayor appealed to the crowd in the name of good sportsmen to consider what the undaunted boxer had gone through in addition to the long journey from London, and allow a clear passage so that he could go home for his well-earned rest. The crowd then diminished, and Basham on rising to acknowledge all, which he did by saluting in military fashion, was greeted with the excited waving of handkerchiefs and hats, and the car went its way to the accompaniment of "For He's A Jolly Good Fellow."

CHAPTER X

The Nineteen Rounder

"I Heard A Woman Crying."

This time, Johnny knew it, he could beat Lewis. Indeed, he was so confident of his ability to beat the Aldgate fighter that he was ready to put up one thousand pounds of his own money. The idea of a return bout caught the public imagination and the fight was pencilled in for November 19th, 1920 at the Royal Albert Hall.

Secure in his Wrexham fastness, Johnny set about preparing for the contest. His training methods differed radically from those of other boxers. Instead of spending time on three minutes of ground exercises, ball punching and shadow boxing, he would go through these type of exercises in spasms, in an effort to relieve the deadly monotony of training. Whilst training he would keep up a stream of constant banter with the many spectators. The "Old Guard" took a look at Johnny's training camp and found his sparring bouts to be serious affairs:

"He boxed with all kinds of boys at various weights and got through twenty-one rounds without a break at lightning speed. He looks in grand fettle and is well within the weight. His road work consists of from sixteen to twenty miles every morning and he seems to thrive upon it. Generally, he rests in the afternoon, doing all his work in the morning and at night."

What the "Old Guard" failed to mention was that Johnny's training camp had a secret weapon in the shape of an Airedale dog, given to him by his manager, Will Dodman:

"This intelligent fellow used to watch me at work as if he knew every move on the board. I could always get a big laugh by starting a quick short sprint with the dog after me. Neither faster nor slower would he go, but keep just abreast of me, and when I got back to our starting point I would throw myself down to the mat that would be lying ready for me, and lying on my back proceed to do what is known as ground work, but which army gymnasium and school instructors call Swedish drill.

No sooner had I flopped on my back and started working my legs than the dog did likewise, and although those present always roared with laughter at this performance, the dog took it very seriously, and his look of reproach at those laughing was worth travelling miles to see!"

Meanwhile, Ted Kid Lewis was fighting as hard in the gymnasium as

The Barrack Square, Wrexham, 1920.
Johnny takes a swig of water as he prepares for his second fight with Ted "Kid" Lewis.
His sparring partner is "Battling" Vernon of Moss.

he did in the ring. Unlike Johnny, who was all "fun and frolic", Lewis put his sparring partners through gruelling, two-round "fights" of three minutes each round. Lewis was in first-rate condition when he left America, having fought only a couple of days before leaving for home. He kept himself fit by sparring with all comers on the ship and was not too worried at having to land in England only ten days before the fight was due to take place.

The evening before the fight Johnny arrived at Paddington at 9.25 and went straight to the Strand Palace Hotel. The "Old Guard" had been impressed by his appearance at Wrexham but thought the quality of his sparring partners left something to be desired. The question now was: would Johnny be able to keep Lewis at bay for what were sure to be twenty of the longest and hardest rounds he had ever fought? Could his famed straight left hold Lewis and bring him a victory on points? Ominously for Johnny, the "Old Guard" concluded his pre-fight report by saying that:

"Basham is a clever boxer. So is Lewis. The latter, however, is much the harder hitter of the two."

If such thoughts troubled Johnny, he did not show it as he climbed into the ring, "hair parted neatly in the middle and smoothed flat," his body "dark, lithe and sinewy." By contrast, his opponent was "fair, heavy-shouldered and muscular, with his hair frizzled and his jaw set — a typical fighter." The stage was set for one of boxing's most enduring confrontations: the boxer versus the fighter. Eugene Corri was the man chosen to referee the fight and his was the best view in the house as Johnny took the opening few rounds with crisp, precise straight lefts. At this stage of the fight Johnny was doing everything right: he was avoiding Lewis's dangerous attacks and he was boxing beautifully. Right from the start he had made clear his superiority and was intent on giving Lewis a boxing lesson.

Skilfully, Johnny was piling up the points, yet all the while, he was avoiding Lewis's crafty attempts to mix it. As for Lewis, he was putting up a sound defence, although his fighting methods hid a lot of his undeniable boxing skills from the average onlooker. Time and again he attempted to land his famous short right upper cut, but Johnny made sure he was never at the other end to receive it. In the fifth round the Londoner was "bewildered" by the variety of attacks and "non-plussed" by the speed with which Johnny "landed and was clear" before Lewis realised what was happening.

So far, so good. At this stage of the fight, Johnny's supporters must

A solemn Johnny Basham and Ted Kid Lewis face the camera at the weigh-in for their second fight.

have been fairly confident that it would be their man whose hand was raised in victory, but twenty rounds is a long way to go and, as in life, there is no certainty in boxing. Lewis was nothing, if not tough and wily, and in the sixth he began to get to grips more often. He also began to lean and hold and — although cautioned for this several times — "robbed" Johnny of some of his speed and a lot of his stamina. In the eighth, Lewis rushed his man and fired off a fusillade of lefts and rights which, it seemed, must sink Johnny. But to the great approval of the crowd, the darling of Wales rode the storm and, towards the end of the round, he was giving as good as he got and a little more besides. Nevertheless, during the course of his whirlwind attack, Lewis landed a heavy blow on Johnny's eye and he began to rub it frequently, a sure sign he was in pain. Seeing this, the Kid began to drop his wild swings and uppercuts and concentrate more on boxing. He cut Johnny's mouth and the blood began to flow freely, but despite these successes, Basham was still the master and, try as he might, Lewis was not being allowed to dictate the fight in his usual hurricane fashion.

Then it happened. The blow came in the fatal thirteenth round. Until then, Johnny had been well ahead on points and the fight had seemed to be his for the taking. His left had done its job splendidly and, for the most part, kept Lewis where Johnny wanted him, well out of harm's way. Lewis was not used to such treatment, and the Londoner's seconds were forced to revive their fighter with ice at the back of his skull and a draught of refreshing champagne. All Wales prepared to celebrate but the thirteenth proved unlucky for Johnny. Kid Lewis sent over a right which split the Welshman's left ear. Blood poured from the wound and the whole complexion of the fight was changed completely. Until that blow, Johnny had looked well in command. Now, suddenly, it was Lewis who seemed to hold all the aces. He had a target to aim at and he attacked that target with all the physical force he possessed.

Weakened by loss of blood, Johnny was in great pain and badly shaken from the effects of that tremendous right hand. He was now fighting for his life and there were five rounds to go. If he could only hang on, victory and the title would be his, he was so far ahead on points. But would Lewis let him hang on? The "Dashing, Crashing, Smashing, Bashing" Kid was not the sort of man to show mercy. He expected none himself and gave none to others. He homed in on Johnny's badly wounded ear. In the fifteenth round alone he aimed four heavy blows on the same spot. The more Johnny visibly weakened, the more Lewis hammered away at the cause of all his troubles. Now, more

The Kid attempts to take Johnny's head off, as Eugene Corri looks on.

than ever, Johnny needed to call upon all his reserves of courage and ringcraft. If he could only hold on, his titles would be his again. Desperately, he tried to stop the rampant Aldgate Juggernaut.

Knowing that he could not win on points and that only a k.o. would do, Lewis continued to subject Johnny's left ear to grievous bodily harm. By the time the nineteenth round arrived, Johnny was still in the lead — just — thanks mainly to his earlier display of masterly boxing, but he was now deep in trouble and looking very much the worse for wear. Both his eyes were bruised and his ear and mouth were badly cut. Only his indomitable fighting spirit remained, but Lewis's heavy punches were beginning to take a terrible toll.

When the bell sounded for the start of the nineteenth round, the Kid determined to force the pace. The two men clinched and a weary Johnny failed to raise his guard in time. Seeing his chance, Lewis sent over a left and then a tremendous right which dropped Johnny to the boards. It looked all over. The force of the blow was so great that Johnny staggered and fell heavily to the floor in a sitting position. He then fell on his head. Any ordinary fighter would have stayed where he was but, in the words of "The Old Guard":

"He struggled up, and, catching the ropes, drew himself upright. He retreated round the ring as Lewis approached, trying to repel the expected onslaught. Lewis walked coolly over, and measuring his man, carefully struck several blows. With instinctive cleverness, Basham avoided the full force of these, but Lewis was relentless, and finally got home fairly and squarely on the jaw again. Basham crashed to the floor on his back, still near the ropes. Again his gallant spirit brought him up after a long struggle, but the brave fellow was just too late."

But was he? Confusion now reigned. Many of the crowd thought that the referee had stopped the fight. Will Dodman, Johnny's manager, protested vehemently that his fighter had been up at "six" and beaten the count. Eugene Corri pointed to the timekeeper, Mr. Thwaites, and said that he had counted Johnny out, but to complicate matters still further, Mr. Thwaites denied this, saying that Mr. Corri had stopped the fight. The calmest man in the ring appeared to be Johnny Basham himself. "Never mind," he said, as he walked back to his corner, his excited seconds crowding around him, "Don't blame Mr. Corri, he got mixed up. It's Ted's night out, that's all."

If only, if only ... probably the two most poignant words in the English language. If only Johnny had kept his straight left going to the last; if only Lewis had not landed his blow when he did; if only the fight had

Down goes Johnny in the nineteenth round.

been scheduled for fifteen and not twenty rounds; if only Eugene Corri had allowed Johnny to battle on to the bitter end. So many if onlys. If only Johnny had met Lewis a few years before, when he was truly in his prime. If only... And so on, and so on, forever and a day. But then " If only..." never did win any fights. The cruel reality was that lightning did strike twice in the same place. Once again, Ted Kid Lewis had beaten Johnny Basham.

The next day the headlines in "The South Wales Argus," the paper Johnny had sold on the streets as a boy, read "Strength overcomes British science." Elsewhere the columns of the sports writers were filled with laments for the passing of a great fighter. One typical comment was that Johnny had gone to his defeat like "a true British champion — game, determined to the end." Speaking to the "Evening News," Johnny himself said:

"I feel very disappointed at the result. I was certain in my own mind that I had beaten the count. Well, I am through with the fighting game, and you can take it from me that I shall never box again. It was a hard fight, and of course, I could not say whether I was leading on points or not."

Seven years later, Eugene Corri gave his side of the story on the disputed end of the fight. In "Gloves and the Man", he wrote:

"I might have had some difficulty in naming the winner of the second fight at the Stadium had Lewis not knocked out Basham in the nineteenth. The scales were very evenly balanced till the knock-out tore my card up, so to speak. I told Lewis how close it was, and he said. 'Well, Mr. Corri, I've won. Let it go at that; never mind what might have happened.'"

Ted Kid Lewis was clearly not a man for "if onlys." Even so, most unbiased observers agreed with the Kid that, had the fight continued, Johnny's chances of survival would have been slim indeed. Lewis himself had no doubts that he was a worthy winner. Before sailing to New York, he told the waiting press:

"I could have stopped the fight with Basham in any round. Practically I could have finished the fight when I liked."

Whilst Lewis prepared to leave for America, Johnny returned to Wrexham. Here at least, he was still a hero. The night of Monday, November 21st, 1920 was cold and foggy, but this did not prevent several thousand people turning out to welcome Johnny home. The train was late and the Rhosddu and Acton Silver Band played suitable music to amuse the waiting crowds. When the train did arrive, it was met by the

Mayor of Wrexham and by a "motor chara" which bore Johnny through the town at a snail's pace, so great were the cheering, welcoming crowds. All along the route windows were open as people clamoured to catch a glimpse of the boxer. Preceded by the band and the light of flickering torches the procession made its way to the Wynnstay Hotel.

Here the Mayor received loud applause when he welcomed Johnny as a Royal Welch Fusilier, a fellow-townsman and a Welshman. He congratulated Johnny on being a clean fighter and said that his opponent had fouled him no less than twenty-seven times. Then it was Johnny's turn. When he told the crowd that he was not much of a fellow " at this game of speaking, " he received a tremendous ovation. He went on to thank them from the bottom of his heart for the fine welcome they had given him. He loved Wrexham, and although tempting offers had been made to him to go to the States and Australia, he had always stayed in Wrexham, because the people of Wrexham were of the right sort and had red blood in their veins, and they were all "white" people.

As for the fight, Johnny told the crowd that the result had been a surprise for him, as he had never felt a "beaten boy" all through the contest. It was in the fateful nineteenth round that he happened to hear a woman crying, probably from seeing his ear bleeding, and he looked towards her when Kid Lewis gave him the blow which felled him for the first time. But they had to adhere to the referee's decision.

Johnny's manager, Will Dodman, added that the referee had admitted to him that Johnny had not been knocked out, and the timekeeper had said that he had not been counted out. So the referee had brought the game to a close for reasons best known to himself.

At the beginning of December, Johnny was the guest of honour at a dinner given by Wrexham sportsmen. Even now, the Lewis defeat still rankled. After the Royal Toast, a Captain Ross Willis said that he had seen Johnny's last two fights, and did not know how Lewis could have won at the Albert Hall. Johnny had not been knocked out, but had walked to his seat after rising at the count of "five." Afterwards, when they had been commenting on the result, Johnny had told them to forget it, as Eugene Corri had given the fight to Lewis. *"That, thought Captain Willis, said by a man who had been training for many weeks, and who had been looking forward to the fight, was an indication of Johnny's character which was that of a true sportsman."*

In his speech the Mayor placed Johnny on a par with those two other famous North Walians — Billy Meredith and Lloyd George. Not only could Johnny fight but he fought fair and accepted the referee's

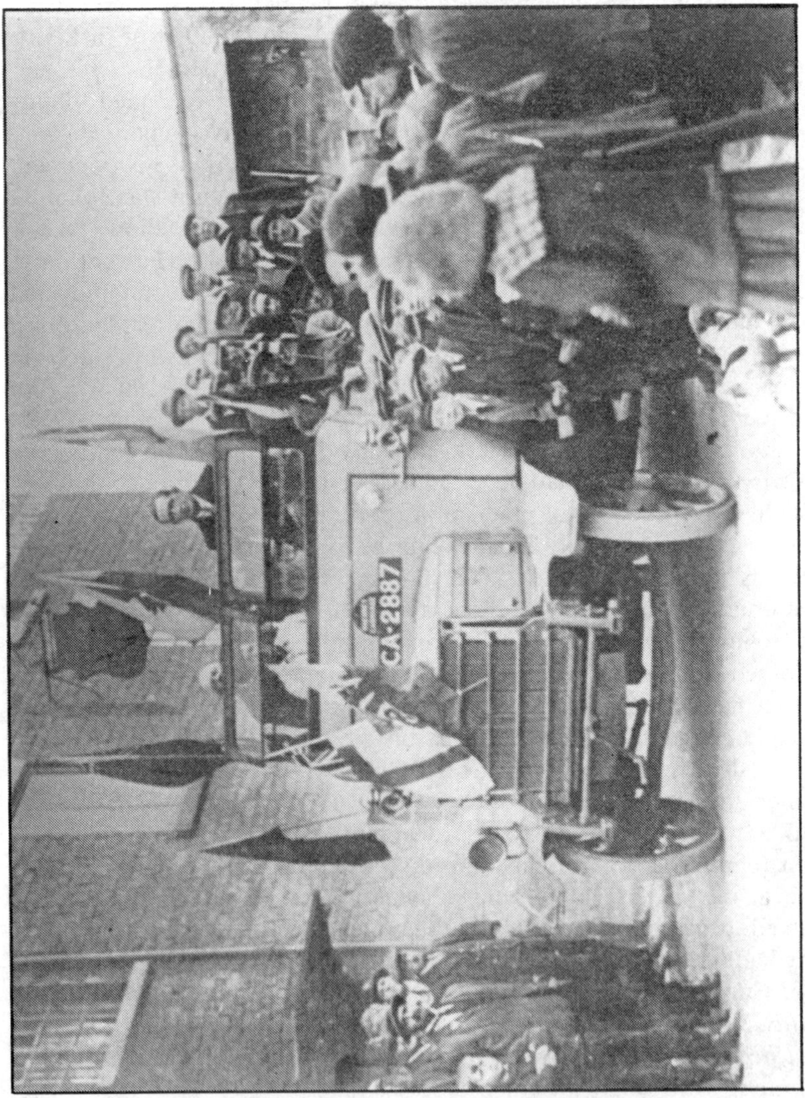

Johnny's "Motorcade" arrives at the Duke of Wellington, Acrefair, North Wales in 1920.

decision, even if he and his friends were confident that he had been winning on points. This theme was taken up by Will Dodman, Johnny's manager, who told the dinner guests that "when his opponent was not running on the straight that they begged of Johnny to adopt like tactics, but he refused, saying that he did not want to win, if he could not win fairly."

CHAPTER XI
Champagne Versus Guinness

"The Third Time Shall Pay For All."

Even after two defeats, Johnny was still convinced he could beat Lewis. In the previous two fights, he and his supporters claimed, he had had to weaken himself considerably to make the weight. Bill Dodman, Johnny's manager, recalled how Johnny had been compelled to walk sixteen miles on the morning of the second fight with Lewis, the "nineteen-rounder." Now that Johnny was boxing as a Middleweight, he felt very much more confident within himself. Lewis was also agreeable to a third encounter and so the two men signed articles to meet at the Royal Albert Hall in October, 1921. As both Lewis and Basham claimed the European Middleweight title, the winner would be crowned undisputed champion.

There was the usual pre-fight manoeuvring. There was talk of Basham going to America to fight Johnny Wilson for the World Middleweight Title, but nothing came of it. Lewis, however, did go to America after beating Jack Bloomfield, and claiming the British Middleweight title. Once in the States, he intended to challenge Jack Britton and would return to England at least three weeks before his fight with Basham, a fight which was to take place under the direction of Major Wilson.

In the event, the Kid did not meet Britton, but landed in Southampton on Friday, October 1st, from the "Berengaria". He told the waiting Press, "Basham is an opponent for whom one has to be fit, or pay the penalty." The reporters were suitably impressed by this, as they were by the Kid's grip, which would not have been out of place on a heavyweight.

Five days later, the "Old Guard" was present as the "Aldgate Juggernaut" worked out at Wembley:

"He punched the ball, skipped, shadow boxed, went through a spell of ground work exercise, and boxed with two sparring partners at a speed which would have left a less fit man badly short of wind."

For his third fight with Basham, Lewis had a new trainer, Jack Goodwin, well known as the man who had trained more champions than any other trainer living. Goodwin was well pleased with his new acquisition. Lewis was a pleasure to train, he said, and added *"Even the best of them get nervy, as the time draws nearer and nearer, but this is not so with*

Ted. The fight seems to be the last thing in his mind, yet it must be the first, as he never slacks up, and never gets jumpy."

After watching Lewis, the "Old Guard" then travelled to Wrexham to view preparations in the Basham camp. He was met by Johnny himself and soon learnt that 300 supporters had booked seats for the fight and intended travelling by train from Wrexham. They would be easily recognisable from the Welsh colours in their coats and their roars of encouragement for Johnny.

Wrexham Drill Hall was packed as Johnny went through his paces. He dealt with as many as fifteen partners in one afternoon, including flyweights and heavies. Clearly showing that he intended to rely on speed to beat Lewis, Johnny danced his way through fourteen rounds, although he twice knocked down his heavyweight partner. He had deliberately done little road work for the fight. During the morning hours he was never still for a second, and considered this to be far better than mile after heartbreaking mile of walking whilst weighed down with heavy sweaters.

Having seen both Basham and Lewis train, the "Old Guard" felt entitled to give his readers the benefit of his speculations regarding the fight. On October 13th, 1921 he wrote that Johnny was :

"The champagne of boxing — all sparkle and bubbles, while Lewis resembles Guinness the stuff that gets you down and worries you. When Basham sparred with his partners and hit them hard, he kidded them to carry on. Not so Lewis who is as ruthless in the gymnasium, as he is in the ring. Major Wilson says there is an enormous demand for tickets. Lewis looks splendidly fit. This is the first time that he has engaged Jack Goodwin but he said 'Goodwin will do me until I am through with boxing.'"

The following day, another newspaperman, "W.W." of the "Daily Express" gave his views on the men of the hour:

"Johnny Basham, however, the darling of Wales, and one of the pluckiest men who ever stepped into a ring is like none of his fellows in the boxing game. He ought to have been a music-hall "entertainer." He is as full of quips and strange jests as Jack Point, and his humour will pop incontinently out in the middle of a round with a sparring partner. The last time he met Kid Lewis he smiled his way through nineteen of the hardest rounds any man ever fought. In the last round he had a badly cut ear and mouth and two discoloured eyes. But he did not lose his smile until the referee stopped the fight. Then he was really vexed.

"Lewis never smiles in the ring — a fighting machine, his massive

How Johnny made the third time "pay" for all.

shoulders would not disgrace a heavyweight. Lewis is built for fighting — his arms too. He's not pretty but magnificent to watch when boxing. Also terrifying. He moves towards his opponent with a mask like death — his sallow skin seems to turn a "ghastly greenish yellow" when the fight begins and, as the fight develops, the frightfulness of the mask increases. Men who have been defeated by him say that he frightened them out of the fight!"

At the weigh-in, Johnny received a nasty shock. He and his advisers had been convinced that he would be heavier than Lewis, and they were not alone in this view. Even Mr. Keen, the official at the scales, took a few pounds off before taking his seat after Johnny had weighed in at ten stones twelve pounds. He had to get out of his seat to put them back on again as the Kid tipped the scales at eleven stones. According to Jack Goodwin, Lewis's new trainer,

"Johnny looked particularly puzzled, and the onlookers had all sorts of weird explanations for the phenomenon. They had left the trainer out of their calculations. I had built up his muscle for the fight — an art very little understood in the gymnasium."

Goodwin had indeed done a good job on his fighter. When Ted Lewis engaged him as a trainer, he had only ten days in which to get to work. At first Goodwin had been dismayed to see Lewis's hands, the worst hands the trainer had ever seen in a champion boxer, a legacy of course, of the hundreds of hard fights he had had in the United States. Lewis and Goodwin began their preparations for Basham at the Norfolk Arms, Wembley and, after the day's work was over, Lewis would belie his dour ring image by playing cards, dancing to his own portable gramophone, which he always had with him in camp, or perhaps visiting a local music hall or boxing tournament.

When the time came to fight, Lewis had a great send-off from the people of Shoreditch where he was staying at the time, and where the local people idolised him. On the way to the Albert Hall, it was discovered that Ted had forgotten to bring his pass. He was all for turning the car round straightaway, but his friends protested, saying it would be bad luck to turn back. But Lewis believed in making his own luck, and he waved aside their protests and turned back to Shoreditch to collect his pass.

Meanwhile, Johnny Basham waited patiently in his hotel rooms surrounded by a host of good luck telegrams and his mascot. This was the moment of truth and he knew it. Had he not said " the third time shall pay for all?" Could he stop Lewis and revenge his earlier two defeats?

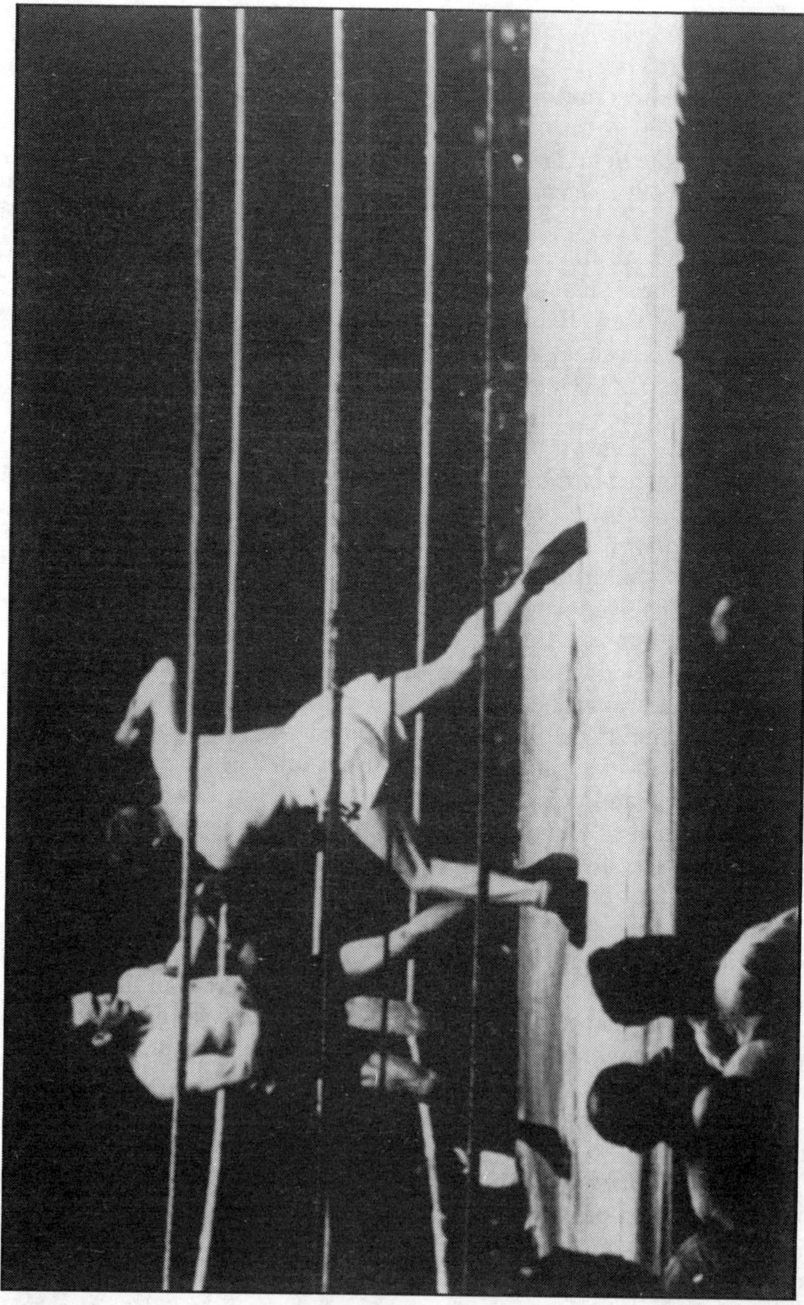

Johnny stands ready to take all that "Kid" Lewis can throw at him.

After the surprise of the weigh-in, the omens were not hopeful. Even Johnny, with his boundless courage and optimistic outlook on life, must have felt the faintest glimmers of self-doubt.

Would it be third time lucky for Basham? The Welsh have a saying — "Three Tries for A Welshman," but, this time, the odds were fully stacked against the "Darling of Wales." He had already lost twice to Lewis and taken some tremendous punishment in the process. Added to that, Lewis was a far more effective puncher than Johnny, youth was on his side and he had, after all, been world champion.

If John Michael Basham felt any qualms along these lines, as he stepped into the ring in front of a packed Albert Hall, he kept them to himself. Wearing the Welsh colours tied round his waist above his dark shorts, Johnny looked "smiling and confident." The Kid, by contrast, looked his usual "pallid" and "dour" self, but he did sport a touch of colour with his white satin shorts and their embroidered monogram. As the referee, Joe Palmer, got the fight under way about ten p.m., the packed crowd held their collective breath. But they were not to be held in suspense for long ... To the consternation of his supporters, Johnny was clearly a beaten man by the end of the first round, having palpably failed to demonstrate any kind of superiority. The Kid came at Johnny like a tornado, fists flailing and bearing down on his man with merciless, thunderous blows. But this time poor Johnny was utterly incapable of holding his tormentor at bay.

Round after round Lewis applied the same remorseless pattern to which Johnny had no answer. He tried to follow Lewis around the ring and be aggressive and forceful, but the Londoner easily tied him up in the clinches. The crowd could hardly believe their eyes. Here was a new Johnny Basham, a Johnny Basham being made to look slow, a Johnny Basham lacking in ringcraft, precision, correct timing and, most important of all, a Johnny Basham without a punch. Lewis seemed to be faster, cleverer and more persistent than Johnny. Worse than that, he was giving Johnny a punching lesson. The third round had shown once again his capacity for delivering killing blows. Once again, the damage was caused by a blow to Johnny's left ear.

But if Johnny was being out-gunned, out-manoeuvred and out-fought, his indomitable spirit refused to give in. If his boxing skills had deserted him just when he needed them most, he still fought on. He fought on, even though he was smeared with blood and his ear was swollen to a prodigious size. Long before the twelfth round, the crowd was screaming for the contest to be stopped. "The Kid's killing him,

Johnny and the "Kid" "mixing it" in their third fight.

killing him," they cried. And the Basham supporters responded, roaring on their hero, "Good Boy, Johnny!" "Plucky Johnny!" "Give it him, Johnny!" "You've got plenty of pluck left Johnny!" they continued to call, even when it seemed that all hope was lost.

As if in answer to his supporters' cries, Johnny rallied occasionally and attempted to take the fight to Lewis. In the ninth, he feinted for a knock out, but it was too woefully slow and easily avoided by the increasingly confident Lewis, who was now not only out-fighting the Welshman but also out-boxing him. By the tenth Johnny's left eye was cut and the clinches only served to aggravate his misery. It was all a long way from the moment in the first round when, caught in a burst of in-fighting in his own corner, he had cheekily winked at his seconds, although even then, Lewis was boring into him with painful lefts and rights to the ribs.

In the eleventh, Johnny went down for a count of seven. He poked Lewis's head back but the left was no longer the magnificent weapon it once had been. There was no sting behind the punch and the chance was lost.. Only Johnny's "sheer pluck" and the instinctive remnants of his ringcraft kept him in the fight at this stage. By the thirteenth, he was obviously "dazed and weak," he was suffering badly from eye and ear wounds, blood was pouring forth from his body, yet, still, incredibly, he went after Lewis. Sadly for Johnny, the punch he aimed at Lewis's jaw made little impression. To everyone but Johnny, his cause was now all but hopeless. He was seen to stagger halfway across the ring and then a compassionate second threw in the towel. For a moment Johnny was angry, but then he shook the Kid's hand heartily and, in his "free and frank" way, admitted defeat.

So, for the third time, "Guinness" triumphed over "Champagne." As Joe Palmer, the referee put it, "Basham sparkled for a while, but as the rounds went on he gave over winking at his seconds, and his happy smile gradually faded away." As for Jack Goodwin, Lewis's trainer, he poured cold water on the critics' theory that Basham had been but a mere shadow of his former self. As far as Goodwin was concerned, it was Lewis's superior tactics and training which had brought the Londoner victory:

" The critics said afterwards that Basham was only a shell of his former self. That was not the case. It was the wonderful improvement in Lewis's condition and tactics which made the difference.

" Basham himself confirmed this view, for when Ted walked over to him after the referee had given his decision he said: ' You are the better

man. You hit me harder tonight than in either of the previous contests. God bless you.'"

Johnny was only thirty years of age — yet now his boxing career was effectively over. Lewis had proved to be the rock on which he would always break. There seemed to be no way back for the ex-champion. The time was coming fast when the bright lights and the cheers and admiration of his thousands of fans would be no more. What would become of the "Happy Warrior" then?

CHAPTER XII

Failure of a Comeback

"I Am Through With The Fighting Game,
And You Can Take It From Me That I
Shall Never Box Again."

After his third demolition by Ted Kid Lewis, Johnny put away his gloves, apart, that is, from a few exhibition bouts, but he did not retire. Then, almost a year after the disaster at the Albert Hall, he stepped into the ring once more. This time, the venue was Sheffield, the date was October 25th, 1922 and the opponent was America's Mike McTigue. Irish born, McTigue had started professional boxing at the age of sixteen. A native of County Clare, he had spent some time working in Sheffield before emigrating to America. One of twelve brothers and sisters, he was fighting in Britain for the first time.

As always, Johnny did his training at Wrexham and he certainly looked the part, impressing onlookers with his high level of fitness. The fight was scheduled to last the full twenty rounds, but despite being in "surprisingly good form" early on, Johnny never made it to the end of the contest. He was giving away both height and reach to McTigue and was at least six pounds lighter than the Irish-American. The end came in the third. Lulling his man into a false sense of security, McTigue sent over a right and the lights went out on Johnny. As the "Daily Express" correspondent put it, "Basham dropped like a log and never moved during the count." Other reporters had seen the writing on the wall and stayed away. "Corinthian" of the "Sporting Chronicle" wrote:

"I refrained from making the journey because I did not want to see Johnny Basham overwhelmed. Mike McTigue is one of the — if not the best middleweight in the world, and his record is imposing enough to make him a much-fancied candidate with Ted "Kid" Lewis. McTigue possesses the punch. Out of eighteen fights in 1921, fifteen were won by the knockout. In fact, his boxing record is one long series of victories.

"Johnny Basham's boxing days are finished so far as championship fights are concerned, and one would not like to see Johnny appearing among the preliminaries. A gamer man never peeled off his shirt, and his fights with Matt Wells and Ted Lewis will live long in the memories of those who witnessed them."

Johnny after the McTigue fight.

"Basham has never earned big money in the ring, and I believe that he has not a wad of wealth for his days of retirement."

Writing for the "Daily Mail," Trevor C. Wignall was even blunter. Lamenting the fact that Johnny had chosen not to retire when he was still at the top of the tree, Wignall mourned the passing of the old champion, at the same time taking him heavily to task for going on too long:

"Basham has not overdone activity; it cannot be said of him that he fought too often. His full total of contests number sixty-four — an average of less than six per year. One scarcely knows where to look for a reason. It is possible, of course, that the punishment he took from Lewis did him considerable harm. He was badly beaten both at Olympia and at the Royal Albert Hall but no one really thought that he would fall quite so quickly before McTigue.

"The pity is that he was induced to emerge from what most people thought was his retirement. Farewells are all right for actors and singers, but they are invariably sad occasions for boxers. The sensible fighter is he who returns to private life when his flag is still high. Their names could be counted off on the fingers of one hand. Basham's finish must have been indicated when his last fight with Lewis was stopped. He cannot find much consolation in the remembrance that he disregarded the warning."

Yet even now, with his pride seemingly in tatters, Johnny could not quite resist the lure of the ring. True, he did not fight all through 1923, but on Monday, November 17th, 1924 he emerged from his semi-retirement to trade punches with Jerry Shea of Newport. The wheel had turned full circle. Johnny was back where he had started all those years ago, when he had taken his first tentative steps up the ladder of boxing in the town where he was born. This fight was not being held beneath the bright lights of the Olympia, or the NSC ring at Covent Garden, nor indeed at his old "home" ground of the Liverpool Stadium. This time the fight was at Newport's Stow Hill Pavilion and the show was in aid of the town's Royal Gwent Hospital.

The name of Jerry Shea was a famous one — but its owner had won undying fame not within the confines of the roped square, but upon the rugby field. Jerry was a competent boxer who had "mixed it" with some of the best men of his day but he had been no match for Ted Kid Lewis ,who knocked him out after only sixty-two seconds. If the truth be told, rugby was more in Jerry's line. Give him a rugby ball and he was dynamite. He had proved that many times — for Pill Harriers, Newport RFC and, on one never-to-be-forgotten occasion for Wales. Against England at Swansea in 1920, Jerry Shea defeated the opposition almost single-handedly. Sixteen of the nineteen Welsh points were scored by Jerry — two dropped goals, one conversion, one penalty goal and one try. No wonder they called it "Jerry Shea's match." He was also a fine athlete and swimmer and had played rugby league for Wigan. His fight against Basham was to be his last appearance in the professional ring.

As things turned out, he at least would finish his boxing career on a high note. Johnny Basham had prepared especially for the fight in London and now, on the Monday afternoon of the fight, he weighed in at eleven stone four pounds whilst Shea tipped the scales at eleven stones three pounds. Both men were said to be the best of friends and, as Johnny took his turn on the scales, he turned to Shea and remarked jocularly, "See you tonight, Jerry."

Johnny would not have been human if he had not entertained thoughts of a comeback but the scheduled fifteen-rounder, although it went the distance, brought him little comfort. Far from being a fairy-tale return to his home town it only confirmed what many good judges had long feared — the old magic was gone forever. Even the presence of his friend and mentor, the legendary "Peerless" Jim Driscoll, now grey-haired and ageing, in his corner could not inspire the "Happy Warrior" to turn back the years.

The large crowd that had paid their money to see two local sporting heroes in action were witnesses to a sad sight. The Basham they saw in the ring that night was but a pale and ineffectual shadow of his former brilliant self. There was no trace of the man who had reigned supreme over all other welterweights for six years. Johnny's lightning-fast speed, once his greatest asset, had left him completely. He was bereft of his punching power. His judgement and ring craft had vanished, as if they had never been.

Against the combined forces of Jerry Shea and advancing "old age," there could be only one outcome. From start to finish, it was the rugby-playing boxer, the great all rounder who dictated the course of the fight, not the ex-welterweight champion of Great Britain. Try as he might, Johnny could hardly win a round. Saddest of all, the once great champion was reduced to clinching and holding for most of the fight. So the clash of the native Newportonians ended in defeat for Basham and victory on points for Shea.

It was left to the "South Wales Argus" reporter present at the fight to write Johnny Basham's sporting obituary:

"Those who knew Johnny Basham at his best sighed with relief when the last bell sounded. Johnny has lost his judgement, keenness of eye,

Jim Driscoll, Johnny's friend and mentor.
Driscoll seconded Johnny in his last fight in Wales.

punching power, quickness and precision. It was a pitiable sight to find him allowing Jerry Shea to lead, lead, lead; it was tragic to see this one-time master of strategy, ringcraft and aggression made the pupil of one who could never have held a candle to him in the days of his greatness."

Even Johnny, it seemed, could not buck one of boxing's oldest truths — "They Never Come Back". As his career had started, so, too, did it finish, in a boxing ring in a small hall in Newport. The ghost of the "singing boxer" had come back to haunt him.

CHAPTER XIII

Into The Twilight

"I Made Plenty of Money,
But Thought Nothing Of
It — Nor Do I Regret It Now."

What does a boxer do when his legs no longer respond, his punches lose their sting and his ring-generalship deserts him? If he is wise, he gets out while the going is good, having taken the precaution of putting by a tidy sum for his old age. Johnny had failed on both counts: the "comeback" fight with Jerry Shea had shown that there was no future for him in boxing, no way back to the commanding heights of the fight game. As for putting some money by, Johnny was no business man and, in the days of plenty, he had been generous, too generous to those around him. He now faced an uncertain future. He was thirty-four years of age. What was he going to do with the rest of his life?

He began by spending three months in Holland training the Dutch Olympic Boxing Team and, at a chance meeting with the "Old Guard", let it be known that he would like a crack at Johnny Brown, of Hamilton, — fifteen or twenty rounds — Johnny Basham was not fussy. The offer, if such it was, was never taken up — instead Johnny now embarked on an odyssey of different jobs, boxing in exhibitions, boxing in booths, doing the occasional piece of work and wandering the country in search of permanent employment.

It was a bad time to be cast adrift. Johnny's fall from grace coincided with the depression years. 1926 was the year of the General Strike, 1929 that of the Wall Street Crash. In the words of the Monmouthshire poet, Idris Davies, the "great dream" was followed by the "swift disaster".

For the rest of 1924 and throughout 1925, 1926 and 1927 Johnny kept busy with two and three-round exhibition matches. But now the venues were no longer the Liverpool Stadium, the National Sporting Club or the Albert Hall.

Johnny had come home. He had returned to his Welsh working class roots. He fought now at Caldicot Working Men's Club, Newport Cattle Market Stadium, Pillgwenlly Labour Hall, Bargoed New Hall, Pontypool, Pentre, Mardy, Bedwas, Pontypridd and Pandy. The list of places he boxed in reads like a litany of South Wales and the Valleys. Johnny had indeed come marching home but the bright lights of the big city were a fading memory. The fists which had once tapped out so many triumphant victory tatoos now merely went through the motions.

As always, however, Johnny tried his best. He attempted to make a go of it as a fireman in London, but on the sixth of June, 1928 the headlines read:

"Fireman Johnny Basham, the ex-welterweight boxing champion is lying unconscious in St. Bartholomew's Hospital following an accident while he was practising with hook and ladder at Cannon-Street fire station. Doctors reported his condition late last night as 'still serious'. He is suffering from concussion."

His career as a fire-fighter over, Johnny turned for a while to acting. On December 15th, 1928 the "Old Guard" reported that Johnny had been booked to play a part in the cast of "Is Zat So", taking over the role recently held by Jack Perry, the American boxer.

This, too, did not last. 1929 saw a series of articles appear in the "Empire News" under Johnny's name and, amazingly, on December 13th of that same year, he once again faced Ted Kid Lewis for the fourth and final time. Basham was now 39 and Lewis 35 and, ever the optimist, Johnny still thought he could beat his old adversary. He even asked for the scheduled number of rounds to be increased from six to ten. For months past, Johnny had been boxing in booths and he was fully confident that, this time, he would exact full revenge.

When the opening bell rang at London's Hoxton Baths, Lewis looked much the fitter man and it soon became clear that he was far too strong for Johnny. In the second he dropped Johnny for a count of five and gave him a nasty cut over his left eye. In the third the cut was quickly re-opened by another right hand and became a nasty gash. At once the referee stopped the fight, much to the relief of the watching newspaper reporters.

After the Hoxton Baths encounter, Johnny drifted out of the limelight and into obscurity. Occasional sightings were made of him and the odd reporter or boxing critic would contribute a piece on "Whatever Happened To Johnny Basham?" but for the most part, his name was no longer news. One person who did cross his path as he attempted to come to terms with life after his years at the top was the boxing writer, James Butler. In "Kings of the Ring", Butler describes how he happened to meet Johnny one day in London:

"Something familiar in the jaunty step of the figure just ahead, something in the perky poise of the head on the well-set shoulders stirred the

chords of memory and made me quicken my pace down Charing Cross Road.

"I stretched out a hand to tap his shoulder, a question on my lips. And as he swung round to face me the question was answered.

"It was! After all these years — Johnny Basham! Whimsical, wise-cracking, brilliant Johnny Basham, who, in the days of his greatness, met victory and defeat with the same lively smile.

"And now, as he thrust the right hand that once had dealt out such wicked punishment into mine with a delighted 'Hello Jimmy!' that smile was again prominent.

"It was a cheery, expansive grin that suggested that the former welter-weight champion hadn't a care in the world, yet it was more than obvious that life had not been treating him any too generously.

"Johnny's clothes, neat though they were, had seen better days. So, too, had his shoes, while a stubble of beard decorated his chin.

"And, almost as though he had guessed my thoughts, Johnny laughed.

"'You know, Jimmy,' he said, 'I was just thinking how I used to come down Charing Cross Road to draw my cheques from Major Wilson.

"'Now look at me! Yet I'm just as happy as when I had thousands.'"

By 1933, Johnny was behind the bar of a little pub in Consett, County Durham, pulling pints for his old friend, Tom Lancaster, four years undisputed pit men's boxing champion of Great Britain. It was here that "Daily Express" correspondents sought him out twice that year. The first found Johnny in good spirits and eager to reminisce about the past.

"I got my first fight as a kid," he said. "I was passing a boxing booth, which meant nothing to me then, but I was hungry. So I went in and fought. My 'purse' was two shillings and ten pence (almost 15 new pence). That is how I became a boxer."

Surprisingly, Johnny told the reporter that he did not class his three epic contests with Ted Kid Lewis, as being amongst his greatest struggles in the ring — that honour went to an American:

"The greatest battle I ever fought was with Augie Ratner at the National Sporting Club in 1919. We fought twenty rounds and drew. I made plenty of money, but thought nothing of it — nor do I regret it now."

Johnny told the reporter that his precious Lonsdale Belt was in a safe place in a Wrexham bank and was now the property of his little daughter, Betty. Three months later, he had another visit from the press. Henry Rose of the Manchester edition of the "Daily Express," paid a visit to Consett. He found Johnny still at peace with the world or, to use Johnny's own words — "as happy as a king." Unlike other fighters who had squandered a fortune and had nothing left to show for their years of toil in the ring, Rose found Johnny far from bitter and, if anything, rather philosophical about the cards life had dealt him:

"Happy? I should think so. A good home and I'm alive. What more does anyone want?"

As he said these words, Johnny was dancing to and fro, unable to keep still for even a moment, his fighting blood still keeping his body moving to the rhythm of the ring. It all left Henry Rose puzzled, to say the least:

"His spirit is unconquerable. It beats me. I left Basham with two pictures flicking across my mind — a little tap-room in a Consett inn, and an acclaiming crowd across the ring at the National Sporting Club."

It seemed that Johnny had found a safe haven at last in the north-east of England, but it was not to be. In January, 1935 he was reported to be training the boxers of the Royal Fusiliers and, one year later, he was discovered boxing in an Oxford boxing booth. The Special Correspondent of the "Sunday Chronicle" filed his report dateline September 13th, 1936:

"Today at St. Giles' Fair here, I found Johnny Basham in a boxing booth, ready and willing to take on all comers.

"Johnny today is forty-six years old, grey and battle-scarred, but he is as game and as virile as ever.

"I watched him fight.

"Sizing his man up, standing with left arm outstretched, ready to attack or defend, he was still the stylist of old.

"'What about a come-back, Johnny?' I asked.

"'This is my come-back,' he said. 'I've stepped back thirty years, right back to the days of my boyhood, and I'm enjoying it.

"'That's the best come-back of the lot.'"

It was sad and not a little tragic that a once great champion was reduced to trying his luck with all-comers, anxious to win a little fame by flooring Johnny Basham, once the idol of thousands. But then Johnny probably did not feel that way. As he told the reporter, he was, in all probability, "enjoying" his return to the booths. His sunny outlook on life enabled him to take life's blows, both physical and metaphorical, and deflect them, just as he had deflected Ted Kid Lewis's piledrivers all those years before. Johnny was just built that way — when James Butler said to him, *"Why don't you take care of your money, Johnny?*

Battle-scarred, but still defiant, Johnny surveys the world.

Remember, you won't be able to go on fighting all your life." "Sure, Jimmy," was the laughing reply, " I know. But I can always go back to selling newspapers."

But sometimes it seemed as if Johnny really did intend to go on fighting all his life, or, at least, as long as he was able to. In October, 1936, he took part in a six-round exhibition bout at Swansea with Willie Piper, a young local middleweight. A three thousand strong crowd launched into "For He's A Jolly Good Fellow" after Johnny had treated them to a speech, in which he generously praised his opponent. Johnny showed that night that he had not lost all his old cleverness, although, naturally enough, he sometimes found himself getting the worse of it with an opponent who had not even been born when Johnny was still a champion.

The Swansea connection continued when it was announced on November 3rd, 1936 that Johnny had joined the training camp of the Swansea heavyweight, Jim Wilde, in an advisory capacity and it was strengthened still further when, on December 14th, a boxing programme was held in the town on Johnny's behalf.

Meanwhile, Johnny's old friend and former boss, Tom Lancaster, had started a search for the man who had helped him run his County Durham pubs. As he told the Staff Reporter of the "Daily Express," Lancaster had heard that his old army friend was down on his luck and was trying to find and help him. Appealing to the readers of the "Daily Express," Lancaster said:

"I have heard that Johnny is down on his luck. He has still a pal in Tom Lancaster. If he will only write to me he can come back to Consett and help me in the management of my public house. There is a good home waiting for him here."

For seven years Johnny had helped Lancaster manage his hotels in Durham City and Consett before leaving to take up a job as an army boxing instructor in Swansea.

If Johnny did get to hear of his old friend's plea, he never took him up on his offer. By 1937 he was back living in Newport and — still boxing. On Coronation Day, 1937 he took part in a three-round exhibition at the town's Shaftesbury Park. In May he was named as "honorary" boxing instructor to the Tudor Amateur Boxing Club and, in October, he boxed another three rounds in Caerphilly's Virginia Park.

Apart from these exhibition contests and other activities on the fringes of the boxing world, he was described as having "no regular occupation." Johnny had come home but to an uncertain future. He was now forty-seven years of age, his fortune long gone, his years of fame but a fading memory. The portents were not good. Once again, the question loomed — what did the future hold?

CHAPTER XIV

When Johnny Comes Marching Home

"A Good Home and I'm Alive.
What More Does Anyone Want."

For the next ten years, Johnny Basham became a familiar sight on the streets and in the pubs of Newport. With his rolling gait, his "boxer's walk," and his "laughing blue eyes," he was an easily recognisable figure. In the Pill area of the town, where he had come to live, policemen saluted him and, in the town's market, tradesmen gave him legs of lamb and big London haddocks expecting nothing in return, but, even so, life was far from easy. A job was found as a watchman on the gate at the town's Eastern Dry Dock and, on Sundays, Johnny would relive past glories sparring with interested youngsters "down the docks."

Years later, one of those youngsters, Bob Madden, recalled how, even then, it was difficult to hit Johnny: "You couldn't hit him, you couldn't lay a glove on him." Sometimes, in the "Rising Sun," on Newport's Malpas Road, Johnny would perform the old boxing booth trick for interested bystanders. Standing on a handkerchief, he would sway back and forth, head just out of reach, defying anyone to lay a hand on him. Invariably, they tried and, just as invariably, they failed. In the nights, Johnny was a frequent visitor to Newport's many pubs. In one he served behind the bar, in another he helped out — collecting "dead" glasses. Sometimes, if there was trouble, the landlord would tip Johnny the wink and he would act as a kind of unofficial "bouncer." One story tells of an incident during the Second World War when two American soldiers took it into their heads to throw their weight around in a pub near the docks. The landlord called to Johnny and he wasted little time in "sorting them out". Needless to say, when the G.I.s discovered just who it was they had been tangling with, they were suitably chastened and impressed.

Such are the stories, the legends, the half-forgotten memories of Newportonians some forty to fifty years after the event. But whatever the truth of some of these tales, and like all legends of their kind — they contain at least a grain of truth — it was abundantly clear to all who knew him that Johnny's health was suffering. He still attended boxing functions, he was a familiar sight with his Lonsdale Belt at boxing shows

Johnny was generous to a fault and never refused an appeal for help.

up and down the county, but he was, undeniably, in poor health. Blaina born boxer Ron Dibbin was just an eighteen year-old hopeful when he met Johnny on two separate occasions in 1946. Still extremely popular with crowds at boxing shows, Johnny would ask the promoter's permission and then, during the interval, he would file past the chairs, displaying the belt. The paying customers, those in their sixties and seventies, especially, gave willingly of their silver and coppers to Johnny's hat. Ron Dibbin recalls that Johnny cut rather a sorry figure at this time but was still, as he always had been, a gentleman. And he was still generous to a fault. He gave Ron his silver watch chain and silver pencil — the watch he had long since sold.

Two years before, in 1944, Johnny had been present at an Allied services boxing tournament staged at the Newport Athletic Club Grounds and organised by the Monmouthshire County Military and Air Force Welfare Committee. There were nine contests featuring British boxers and four contests featuring Americans. The star of the show was undoubtedly the then heavyweight champion of the world, Joe Louis, but for a few brief moments, at least, Johnny was able to relive past glories as he, in company with Jack Peterson and Jimmy Wilde was introduced to the crowds from the ringside.

But the seconds were counting down on Johnny. Almost his last public appearance was to record an interview for the BBC. The presenter of the programme was the well-known ex-rugby player and sports commentator, G.V. Wynne Jones, whose other guests were Cliff Curvis and Eddie Thomas. Even today, Eddie Thomas, who himself went on to become British Welterweight Champion, and later manager of world champions, still remembers how he bumped into Johnny Basham on their way to the BBC's recording studio in Cardiff. Thomas was struck by Johnny's "laughing blue eyes", something which he feels all champions must have. For Eddie Thomas, Johnny "epitomised all that is best about Welsh boxing". He was a "gentleman".

Four years later, G.V. Wynne Jones himself recalled the programme in his book, "Sports Commentary." Sadly no recording has survived, but something of the flavour of the programme is conveyed in "Geever's" words:

"Talking of Jimmy Wilde, I was once privileged to introduce a programme with two British champions in it. Both Welshmen, they were Jimmy Wilde and Johnny Basham. The latter had held two British championships, the welterweight from 1914 to 1920, and the middleweight which he won in 1921. Looking at these two ex-fighters one could see a

great difference between them. Wilde, although much of the great sum of money he had made at boxing had been lost, was — and is — in comfortable circumstances. But Johnny Basham was a sorry figure, and almost destitute, and, as unfortunately happened, was to die in poverty within a month of his appearing in this programme.

"In the studio at the same time was Joby Churchill, who had been advisor and guide to Tommy Farr. I discussed Johnny Basham's circumstances with Churchill and it was he who told me that Tommy Farr, like Wilde, had looked after himself and was now a prosperous man. Johnny Basham was a charming fellow with a ready wit and always prepared to crack a joke, and I never thought at the time that I rehearsed for five or six hours with these old-time boxers that both Basham and Jerry Shea, who had been a good Welsh champion, would be dead within a couple of weeks."

Too late, as it turned out, steps were being taken to try and alleviate that poverty. Newport Sportsmen's Committee had decided to organise a boxing tournament, the proceeds of which would be used to establish a trust fund, the hope being to provide Johnny with a small pension for the rest of his life. One of Johnny's last acts was to give his written consent to the proposals of the Newport Sportsmen's Committee, but he never lived to see the tournament. On Friday, June 6th, 1947 he was up and about and walking around the town. On the morning of Saturday, June 7th, 1947 Johnny's wife turned to him and said, "Aren't you going to get the meat, John?" There was no reply. Johnny had collapsed and died at his Mountjoy Place home, apparently the victim of a "seizure". He was fifty-six years of age.

As he had been ill for some time, and under medical care and attention, it was thought unlikely that an inquest would be held. His death occurred only eight days before the boxing tournament which might have brought him fresh hope. From all over the country messages of sympathy flooded in. From Wrexham, so long Johnny's headquarters and home, North Wales sportsmen pledged a contribution to the Testimonial Fund. From London, an old admirer of Johnny's skills sent five pounds, leaving it to the committee's discretion as to how best to use it. Eventually, it was decided to continue with the boxing tournament, firstly to keep faith with Johnny and secondly to give the general public an opportunity to show their appreciation of what Johnny had done for British boxing. The money raised would now go to pay for the costs of Johnny's funeral and to help his dependants. Together, three trustees were to administer the fund, which was given the name of the

"Johnny Basham Memorial Fund".

On Wednesday, June 11th, 1947 John Michael Basham, Lonsdale Belt Holder and true British Champion, was brought to his final resting place. Hundreds of sportsmen and ex-soldiers turned out to pay their last respects. Working men, many still in their working clothes, came straight from their place of work to stand at the graveside. As the funeral procession passed through Newport, many streets were thronged with onlookers as the coffin, draped in its Union Jack flag, made its slow and solemn progress toward the St. Woolos cemetery.

Besides the Basham family and immediate relatives, the mourners included many of Johnny's old sparring partners. Jerry Shea was there as was Fred Rowland from Wrexham, a reminder of happier times, and now representing the Wrexham sporting committee, which had contributed £100 to the Memorial Fund. Representatives of Johnny's old regiment, the Royal Welch Fusiliers, were there as, too, were members of the South Wales Borderers, recalling Johnny's earlier association with the First Regiment of the Monmouthshire Territorials, which formed part of the corps of the Borderers. Many well-known boxers also attended, whilst others sent floral tributes.

Unusually for Newport, where traditionally, "gentlemen only" accompanied the coffin on its final journey, on this occasion many women had found their way to the graveside. As the members of the Newport branch of the British Legion, of which Johnny had been a popular member, held their standard aloft, the Monmouthshire Army Cadets sounded the Last Post and Reveille.

It was a sound with which Lieutenant-Colonel J.E.C. Partridge, who had known Johnny when he was a member of his team of boxers cum Physical Training Instructors in France during the Great War, was very familiar. He, together with the other mourners, some of whom represented the British Boxing Board of Control and the Newport Athletic Club, must have reflected on the tragic irony of Johnny's death — coming as it did, just days before the boxing tournament which would have helped to make his life that little bit easier.

It was a Roman Catholic priest, the Reverend John Colbert, Rector of St. Mary's Roman Catholic Church in Newport, who gave the funeral oration at the graveside, but whatever words the Reverend used they could hardly have bettered the memories of Fred Rowland, Johnny's old friend and sparring partner from his Wrexham days. It was left to Fred to find a perhaps appropriate epitaph for Johnny Basham. As Fred would recall years later:

"The trouble with Johnny was that his heart was too big. He could never resist a hard luck story. He gave innumerable fights for charity. He won many thousands of pounds — and gave most of it away. He had too many fair weather friends who turned their backs on him when fortune was less kind. Had Johnny been a businessman he would have died wealthy. Many people in the Wrexham area can thank him for helping them out of difficulty, but few will acknowledge this. A fool to himself, to others he was the Good Samaritan."

But perhaps we should remember Johnny when he was still in the pride of his youth, doing what he did best — boxing — at a time when he was free of those two implacable assailants ill-health and poverty, and when Trevor C.Wignall could still say of him:

"In action, he was as pretty as a picture; he had so perfected himself that he was able to make boxing as attractive as a ballet. His footwork was perfect, while the ease with which he showered blows on his opponents was of that remarkable kind that induces spectators to imagine that to score with equal facility would be simplicity itself; he resembled Cinquevalli when that wonderful juggler was balancing billiard-balls on the edge of a cue. Most people thought they could do the same without ceasing to breathe, but I never encountered one that could do so.

"Basham was like that. He turned boxing into an affair, that to the observer, was child's play. He juggled with his antagonists as Paul Cinquevalli did with his ivory balls. But he made one sorry mistake; he attempted to out-wit nature after nature had called a halt. He should have said his farewells to the ring after his fine contest with the Australian southpaw, Fred Kay, but instead he went on too long, and was consequently walloped to a standstill on three occasions by Ted Kid Lewis. Basham's exit was somewhat inglorious because he would not admit that his day was done... If Basham had packed up his kit in 1920 he would have been saved from a number of hidings that helped largely to spoil his record, but despite that he still deserves to be selected as one of the world's greatest welterweights."

CHAPTER XV
After The Funeral

Nowadays, if a fading or forgotten pop star dies it often has the effect of boosting the sales of his records. In Johnny's case his death increased demand for ringside tickets at the boxing tournament. Many well-known British boxing personalities, including Nel Tarleton, Peter Kane and Ernie Roderick, pledged to make an appearance and Freddie Mills was due to be introduced from the ring. There were to be five eight-round contests and one six-round bout. Tickets ranged in price from forty-two shillings (£2-10) at the ringside and thirty shillings (£1-50) at the second ringside, down to ten shillings (50p) and five shillings (25p) for the unreserved seats.

On the night of the tournament, Monday, June 16th, 1947 two thousand spectators crowded into the Newport Corporation Repair Depot on Corporation Road. Together they observed a two-minute silence in honour of Newport's finest ever boxing champion. Amongst those taking part in the contests was Merthyr's Eddie Thomas, the same Eddie Thomas who had so recently been firing questions at Johnny Basham in G.V. Wynne-Jones's BBC radio programme. Later that year, in December, it was announced that the boxing tournament had realised a total of £721 for Johnny's widow.

There remained the question of what to do with the Lonsdale Belt. All through his darkest days, Johnny had held on to the belt which had first been presented to Young Joseph in 1910 by Lord Lonsdale himself. It had belonged to Johnny for close on 33 years. Those who saw it say that it was extremely heavy, made of gold, and, in the centre, enamel with its two boxers depicted in a fighting pose. Those who had tried it on for size certainly knew it was there. Even when right down on his luck, Johnny never sought to sell the belt, but its hiding place would raise a few eyebrows nowadays — kept as it was under the damp coal in the coal house. When he took it out to boxing shows and exhibitions, it was always kept wrapped in a blue and white scarf inside a battered cloth case.

Johnny of course had been the third man to own the belt as Johnny Summers had won it twice in June and in December, 1913. Now, with Johnny Basham dead, the belt began to embark on an odyssey of its own. Johnny's widow was the first one to sell it. The buyer was the

Working on the new headstone for Johnny's grave.

Reform Club in Newport of which Johnny had been a member. They held on to it for a while, putting it on display once a year, before selling it in their turn to Joe Carr, a Newport newsagent, who promptly insured his new possession for £1,250. (When Lord Lonsdale first commissioned the original Lonsdale Belts from the firm of Mappin and Webb they cost approximately £250 each.)

Eventually, Joe Carr announced that he was ready to sell the belt to the highest bidder and, in March 1954, he sent it to the London firm of Christie's to be auctioned. It was placed on auction on March 31st, 1954 and was lot number 119 in that particular sale. The catalogue described the belt as follows:

"THE LONSDALE GOLD CHALLENGE BELT, for the British Welter-weight Championship, 1910-1916. With large oval central plaque enamelled with boxers and the Royal Arms above and chased below with sprays of oak foliage, on either side smaller plaques of boxers exercising and beyond this three inscribed medallions of the various matches, the whole joined by openwork links, and backed by red, white and blue silk ribbon, — thirty three and a half inches long."

.The belt was sold with its original mahogany case. Amongst the other lots that day were a Russian silver-gilt square cigarette box, a Viennese gold and enamel statuette and an Austrian gold oblong snuff-box. When the bids were over, the coveted symbol which John Basham had trained so tirelessly for and fought so hard to win and retain, was knocked down for £546. The new owner was Mr. C.H. Nicholls, chief timekeeper to the British Boxing Board of Control, and a man who had officiated at many of Johnny's fights.

Johnny's Lonsdale Belt is now thought to be in America and, thirty-four years after the original auction sale, Christie's are unable to give any information on the identity and whereabouts of the present owner or owners. What is certain is that the Belt is lost to Wales and to Britain. In our present inflationary climate, who knows what price it might fetch if ever it were to come on to the open market again.

Meanwhile, back in his home town of Newport, the man who had won the belt was in danger of being forgotten. A newspaper report in 1951 highlighted the lack of any markings on Johnny's grave and lamented the fact that, without the assistance of the Cemetery Superintendent, it would have been impossible to find it, as it did not even bear his name. There was only a grass-covered mound with an empty vase and two glass shades over some faded, artificial flowers. Yet, as the newspaper reminded its readers "little more than thirty years ago he was

The wooden cross which formerly marked out Johnny's grave.

greeted and applauded everywhere, a highly popular fellow, and no one ever appealed in vain to Johnny for a 'touch'."

Eventually, a simple wooden cross was placed over the grave, but gradually its gilt lettering began to fade. In time, it, too, would have become unrecognisable, but in 1987, Newport's boxing community came to the rescue. It was decided to hold a boxing tournament between a team of amateur boxers from the town and a German team from Heidenheim, Newport's twin town, the proceeds to go towards buying a proper headstone for Johnny's grave. Former Welsh amateur champion, Colin Waters, and Councillor Dick Murray were amongst the organisers and the boxing tournament cum dinner duly went ahead at the Newport Leisure Centre on June 15th, 1987. A special commemorative plate, detailing Johnny's achievements, was commissioned and auctioned to raise funds. Happily, enough money was raised and a firm of Cardiff monumental masons was engaged to carry out the work. In December, 1987 the handsome new headstone was inaugurated at a public ceremony. The inscription reads:

John Michael Basham

Johnny Basham

Born Sept. 13th 1890
Died June 7th, 1947

British Welterweight Champion
1914 -1920

British Middleweight Champion
1921.

The new headstone is inaugurated.

CHAPTER XVI

What They Said About Johnny Basham

DENZIL BATCHELOR: Johnny Basham was a welterweight to be proud of.

B. BENNISON: Johnny Basham, a rare specimen of a welter.

A.F. BETTINSON: Johnny Basham, the Welshman, was another splendid welter-weight. I doubt whether Ted "Kid" Lewis would have beaten him when he was in his prime.

A.F. BETTINSON AND B. BENNISON: Basham, probably the most stylish welter we have had for more than a generation, a boxer supreme, a credit to his profession, and most likeable of fellows.

"BOXING": (comparing Johnny to Augie Ratner): Basham, on the other hand, was as usual all wire and set on wires.

FRANK BUTLER: Basham was a good-looking fellow and a delightful boxer to watch.

JAMES BUTLER: A good-humoured, laughing playboy of the ring.

HARRY CARPENTER: There was never a more inappropriate surname for such a skilled tactician.

NORMAN CLARK: He was not only very fast, and a highly correct and clever exponent of the English style of boxing, but at his best he carried a knock-out punch, and was withal a very game man and a thoughtful ring-general.

"CORINTHIAN": Johnny Summers once foolishly thought that Basham did not possess a punch capable of making a dent in a slab of margarine.

"CORINTHIAN": He is one of those boxers — they are not many — whose skill is so great that one can sit down for long and fail to find a fault.

"CORINTHIAN": He who can beat champions easily is, indeed, a champion. That is the way with Sergeant Johnny Basham, who has placed himself upon a boxing pedestal so high that it is hard to get at the altitude.

EUGENE CORRI: Basham is without exception the hardest man I have ever seen. He never seems to spare himself and never seems to tire himself. On the call of "Time" after each round, he rushes at his man, coming up with him before he has well left his corner. It is the same in the later as well as the earlier stages of the fight, and anyone coming into the audience as Basham left his corner for the fifteenth round might have imagined it was the first round, so energetic was his attack, leading off with his left hand according to his invariable habit.

EUGENE CORRI: Johnny Basham ... was one of the cleverest boxers who ever lived.

EUGENE CORRI: In ordinary clothes you would never take Basham for a champion, but once in action, the merest novice could see that here was a man of real class.

W. BARRINGTON DALBY: Basham fought a really intelligent battle that night (against Summers at the N.S.C.) and he subsequently proved himself to be, if not the greatest welterweight this country ever produced, at any rate certainly the most stylish.

FRED DARTNELL: Basham was always smiling, and I have known him, a few minutes before entering the ring for his painful struggle with Kid Lewis, keep his assistants and friends in the dressing room convulsed with laughter over his witticisms.

GUY DEGHY: The reputedly "exceptionally handsome" Johnny Basham eventually made the Welterweight Lonsdale Belt his own.

"GOAL": Inside and outside the roped square, he is a gentleman.

JACK GOODWIN AND B.J. EVANS: Johnny Basham was very fast and remarkably skilful in the orthodox way — a Driscoll on a larger scale. Unfortunately, he never had a really "kicking" punch, or he would have been invincible.

JACK HAILS: It will be for his great contribution to boxing that Basham will be best remembered.

ALAN HOBY: He was one of the last of the old Corinthians.

NORMAN HURST: He was always ready to laugh and make others laugh. Yet, as a fighter, he was one of the greatest ringsters this country has ever produced.

"JMD": In the ring and out of it Basham's conduct has ever been like his boxing — clean, direct, virile.

JAMES W. KENYON: Johnny Basham, who was known as "Puck in Boxing Gloves."

TED KID LEWIS: Basham is the greatest man I ever fought.

"LSD": Basham is a Welsh Celt, whose twinkling eyes smile when he takes a punch and give the impression that he loves boxing for boxing's sake.

GILBERT ODD: He was a stand-up British-style boxer of great class and ability — a joy to watch.

JOE PALMER: Johnny Basham is of that rare type who will die fighting rather than show the white feather.

JOE PALMER: He was one of the wits of the profession, as well as one of its brightest ornaments, and often his good-natured chaff lessened the bitterness of the pill of defeat for his opponents.

TOM WEBSTER: The lovable Johnny Basham who started footwork where Pavlova left off.

TREVOR C. WIGNALL: He was so brilliant as a boxer that he made most of his opponents ... look like selling platers.

TREVOR C. WIGNALL: His methods were so clean, so crisp, so splendidly thought out. He was the typical British boxer from the soles of his feet to the crown of his head.

A boxing tournament with Newport's twin town of Heidenheim helped raise money for a new headstone for Johnny's grave.

CHAPTER XVII
A Summing Up

Re-reading the foregoing pages again, I am struck most forcefully by two facets of Johnny's personality: his generosity and his sense of humour. Both were legendary. In his time he turned out for such diverse charities as the Cwmbran Catholic Church, the Jim Driscoll Fund, Nazareth House in Cardiff, Newport Catholic Charities, Newport "Poor Cripples" Society, Newport Tramwaymen's Club, St Michael's School Rebuilding Fund, the Sheffield Branch of the National Federation of Discharged Sailors and Soldiers and the Wrexham War Memorial Infirmary Fund.

Examples of Johnny's generosity are legion. Norman Hurst recalls paying Johnny the £25 he owed him on a deal they had had in the Strangers Room of the NSC:

"With him was Tommy Lancaster, the Pitmen's champion. As the pair walked down the club steps, a couple of old-timers said: 'Good luck, Johnny.' He tossed them a pound each! And I will wager that before he reached the end of King Street he had given away a tenner!"

Back home in Newport, Johnny would descend upon his relatives in Maesglas, arms laden with gifts, and shower the children with fruit, sweets and comics whilst all the men in the street came out to shake his hand. In Shaftesbury Street, the old women waited at their door for the pound Johnny would give them, and it would probably be the same old women in their shawls Johnny would take into the Rising Sun later that night for a drink.

So free was Johnny with his money that the people of Newport were said to 'worship' him. Perhaps his generosity came from remembering the hard times he himself had known as a child when, as the son of 'poor but honest' parents, he had taken it in turns with his brothers, Sam and Billy, and his sisters, Kate, Rose, Nellie, Anne and Winnie to sit at the trestle table and eat from the big pot.

And that impish sense of humour? Again tales abound of Johnny's own special brand of fun. There was the time he took his friend and sparring partner, Fred Rowland, down to Cardiff. Now Johnny had presented Fred with a gold watch chain Albert, inscribed with the words 'From Johnny to Fred, December 14th, 1914,' the date, of course, of Johnny's first Lonsdale Belt win. Naturally enough, Fred was very proud of his keepsake and took great care of it.

Johnny had promised to show Fred some of Cardiff's 'tougher' areas and, as they approached a group of people, told him to show them his medal. Fred looked down, but to his horror, his prized possession had vanished! He need not have worried, though. It was just another of Johnny's tricks, to show Fred just how 'smart' some of those Cardiffians were.

The arch joker could also take a joke against himself. Whilst still a Welch Fusilier, he was training for his fight against Chesterfield's Tom Mitchell at the Liverpool stadium, when an old soldier took him aside and said:

"'See here, Basham, I have seen some good men in my time, and some of 'em have told me some good things — now buy me a pint, and I will tell you the biggest secret of all, how to keep clear of the knock-out punch when in the ring.'"

"Whoever heard of such a wonderful secret at such a price? A pint of canteen beer! Why, there were champions to whom such a secret was worth a fortune, so I literally dragged that old-timer to the canteen bar and told the man behind the bar to fill him a pint, whilst I waited impatiently to hear this great thing."

"The old fellow blew the froth off his pint, took a deep draught, wiped his moustache on the back of his hand, and then started his tale: 'I have seen 'em take punches on the nose, on the jaw, and in the eye, I have heard people say — 'Isn't he a game 'un?' but all that can be avoided, if you follow the teachings of Jem Mace —'"

"'And what was that?' I asked, my tongue literally hanging out to know."

"'Well,' said this wise man, with exasperating slowness, 'all you have to do is SHIFT YOUR HEAD!'"

"He had drunk his beer and walked out before I recovered from the shock, and even then what could I do except grin at the way I had been had."

So Johnny was on the receiving end that time, but usually he would be "dishing it out", more often than not with his great friend, Jim Driscoll:

"Jim was always ready to be up to any sort of devilment, and if the joke meant taking a rise out of some swelled-headed fellow that tickled Jim down to the ground.

"At the time I am speaking about Jim and I, together with several racing men, were staying at a big hotel in London. We hadn't been there very long before we learned that an American gentleman on the same

floor as Jim and I had our room was in the habit of giving the pageboy a clip under the ear if he did not jump as actively as he wished him to.

"One of the boys, a big well-made lad, resented this, but, of course, did not say what he wanted to as it would have meant losing his job.

"After listening to the boy's tale of woe for quite a while, Driscoll turned to me and said: 'We ought to do something about this, Johnny. We can't have these fellows coming over here messing our boys about,' so with that Jim ordered drinks while we thought some plans out to punish the gentleman who passed his time bullying the bell boys.

"'I have it,' said Jim, 'come with me' and with that off we went to the boy who had told us the tale. Just a few minutes whispered conversation, and having ascertained that the gentleman with the ready fist might ring at any moment, James Driscoll slipped into the big boy's uniform, plastered his hair well back, and stood ready for action.

"I nearly swallowed two pocket handkerchiefs trying to stifle my laughter as I saw Driscoll parading up and down in that little short jacket, and if that much-waited bell had not rung I would have exploded!

"Up to the door marched Jim, while I trod close on his heels. The boy stopped in his little service room, I suppose trembling and wondering how it would all work out. Jim knocked at the door. 'Come in,' barked a voice, but Jim stood there, and after a second knocked again. 'Come in! What the hell!' and with that the door was wrenched open and we saw our man, though he only saw Driscoll, for I was hiding behind a corner in the corridor.

"'Didn't I tell you to come in? Are you deaf?' said the fellow, and made an open-handed slap at the supposed boy. He hit nothing, and recovering himself made another slap. 'You mustn't strike me, sir,' said the 'boy'.

"Boiling with rage, the bully felt that he was being laughed at, and this time made a terrific drive for Driscoll's head, saying something about impudent pups. Jim's head wasn't there when his fist arrived.

"Something hit him in the waistcoat; something else hit him on the chin, and when he came round Driscoll was seated in one chair with his page's jacket undone, and I was in another chair, and we were both enjoying a drink of Master Bully's wine, which we had found on his table!

"He looked up; he spluttered; he cursed, and then being told who Driscoll was, and what to expect if he dared report anything, he changed his tune and from that time on the page boy at that hotel could go to his room in safety."

Johnny was, of course, famed for his witticisms and most of these have now been lost, but one has survived: after appearing at the Liverpool stadium, a Welsh boxer was found desperately searching amongst his clothing. Asked what he was doing, he replied that he was looking for his waistcoat. Johnny gave him a long look and said, "But you're wearing it." Surprise slowly spread over the Welshman's face as Johnny's words sank in. "Why, you're right," he said. "Now, if you hadn't told me, mun, well, I'd have gone home without it."

Johnny's generosity was not confined to the giving of money. Whilst serving at the Park Hall Camp, Oswestry, during the Great War he stepped in for a fellow soldier who was having trouble with a big Canadian and gave the North American a boxing lesson.

Not that Johnny was a saint by any means. He wasn't — who is? In his early years he had some minor brushes with the law. On Wednesday, August 28th, 1912, he appeared before Newport Police Court charged with loitering in Shaftesbury Street 'for the purpose of betting and receiving and settling bets' and with him, a certain Albert E. Neill for aiding and abetting.

A P.C. Cook, keeping observation in Shaftesbury Street on August 20th, claimed to have seen Johnny receive slips of paper from eight men between 1.40 and 1.55 p.m. At 1.58 he saw Neill come from the Castle Hotel. Basham took a handful of slips from his pocket and gave them to Neill who returned to the hotel. Both men were known to be betting bookmakers.

For the defence, Mr John Moxon said that P.C. Cook had been hiding in the old Castle buildings, inside the brewery ruins, and watching through a boarded-up window, right opposite the Castle. The witness knew that Basham was a boxer — 'and a bookmaker,' interjected P.C. Cook.

"You are a noted bookmakers' detective," continued Mr Moxon "and especially employed upon these cases?" "Yes, sir," said the constable to general laughter.

Mr Moxon said that the men were not giving Basham betting slips at all, but only talking to him about a forthcoming fight in Liverpool. The case was bound to fail as there was no evidence to show that Basham had received any slips either for himself or any other person.

Unimpressed, the magistrates ruled that the case must proceed and Basham himself took the witness stand. He said he was a professional boxer and, a few days after the events in question, had fought in Liverpool and won. He had never, on August 20th, received, made or settled any bets. He did, occasionally, get and settle bets for other bookmakers

STAR EVENTS OF THE WEEK.

LIVERPOOL STADIUM.

THURSDAY, FEBRUARY 19, 1914, at 8 p.m.
GREAT RETURN INTERNATIONAL CONTEST. Fifteen 3min. Rounds.

PRIVATE BASHAM

(Royal Welsh Fusiliers). The Fistic Machine. Liverpool's Favourite. Accepted by the N.S.C. as the next contestant for the Championship and Belt. The cleverest, quickest, and most attractive of the welter-weights. Has beaten Young Ahearn, Badoud (twice), Eddie Beattie, Frank Madole, Tom Tees, etc. Drew with Tom McCormick. V.

YOUNG NIPPER

(Bermondsey). The Cast-iron Welter-weight. Winner of over 200 contests. Knocked out Basham in 5rds. last March. Went 20rds. to a close decision with Johnny Summers at Liverpool. Has beaten Sid Burns (17rds.), Jack Morris (3rds.), Jim Prendy (3rds.), Jack Meekins (twice), Sam Lucas (twice), Jack Langdon (twice). Drew with Arthur Evernden (15rds.) and Matt Wells (10rds.).

Both men weigh-in 10st 7 2 o'clock day of contest. In the ring 9 o'clock.

FIFTEEN 3MIN. ROUNDS CONTEST FOR SIDE-STAKE AND PURSE.

Eddie Jones (Blackburn) v. Kid Eastwood (Brighouse), who box for £15 a-side, deposited with the management, and Stadium Purse.

TWO SPECIAL TEN 3MIN. ROUND CONTESTS.

Young Carnea v. Owen Moran. Harry Groom v. Tom Thomas.

Also other Contests.

Admission: 1s. to 5s. Doors open 7.15 p.m. Telephone: Royal 647.

Boxing! Boxing! Boxing!

RECORD HOLIDAY PROGRAMME.
"Nothing but the Very Best."

AMERICAN SKATING RINK, CARDIFF.

MONDAY EVENING, AUG. 4TH, at 8 o'clock sharp.

BILLY AMES presents his THIRD MAMMOTH

Boxing Tournament.

Great Special Fifteen Rounds Contest:

Private JOHNNY BASHAM v. ARTHUR DUNCAN

(Newport. Coming Welterweight Champion of Eugland). (London. The hardest hitting Welterweight in Eugland).

Special Ten Rounds Contest:

BILLY MARCHANT v. WALLY PICKARD

(Manchester. Featherweight Champion of the North). (Newmacket. "The Fighting Jockey.")

Important Ten Rounds Contest:

JIMMY WILDE v. DARKEY SAUNDERS

("The Tylorstown Terror"). (London).

And Two Special Six Rounds Contests.

Popular prices of admission: 1/-, 2/-. Reserved: 3/-, 5/-, 10/6. Secure your tickets early. Doors open at 7 o'clock to Ticket Holders. No money taken at doors before 7.30.

The Greatest Gathering of Talent ever seen in one programme in Wales.

Star Events of the Week

PREMIERLAND.

COMMERCIAL ROAD, E.

The Largest and most Up-to-date Boxing Arena in England.
Under the Personal Direction of HARRY MORRIS.

SATURDAY NEXT, MARCH 14th.

IMPORTANT 15-ROUNDS CONTEST.

KID LEWIS

(Feather wt. Champion of England)

v.

HARRY BERRY

(Of Ireland).

EXTRA SPECIAL 10-ROUNDS CONTEST.

JACK MORRIS

v.

BILLY WILLIAMS.

Special 10-Rounds Contest.

DIXIE BROWN v. TOMMY LEWIS.

Also several Six-Round Contests.

Prices —
Gallery, 1s.; Ring Seats, 2s.; Stage Seats, 3s. and 5s.

LIVERPOOL STADIUM

THURSDAY, MARCH 12, 1914, at 8 p.m.

SENSATIONAL ATTRACTION.

GREAT WELTER-WEIGHT CONTEST.
15 3-MINUTE ROUNDS.

PTE. BASHAM

(the coming welter-weight champion, who will shortly be matched for a Lonsdale Belt contest)

v.

DICK NELSON.

(the "Fighting Dane," who has met and defeated some of our best welter-weights).

ALSO OTHER SPECIAL CONTESTS.

Admission: 1s. to 5s. Doors open 7.15 p.m. Booking Office (no fees) 10 to 5. Telephone—Royal 647.

SCOTLAND'S BEST CLUB.

VICTORIA A.C.

377, Dalmarnock Road, Glasgow.

On Monday, February 23rd,

JACK TURNER (Scottish Light-wt. Champ.) v. EDDIE BEATTIE, for Welter-wt. Championship and Massive Belt.

Also Other Contests.

Some of the bills advertising Johnny's performances in the ring.

but he did not, and had not, worked for Neill. He had never given a bundle of slips to Neill. From first to last, the police had not spoken to him about the offence. It was untrue to say that eight or nine men had given him slips of paper.

He had come from his Crindau home to the Castle Hotel just before 2 o'clock and had never stood outside the hotel for fifteen minutes. Several people had stopped and asked how he was going to get on in the fight. He did not enter the hotel and again denied any connection with Neill.

Neill himself denied receiving any slips from Basham. He had never employed him this year or last and had finished with him about two years ago. Yes, he was a bookmaker but had not seen Basham on that day until about 3.30. He never employed anyone to receive slips or money for him. A witness confirmed Johnny's story and the magistrates retired to consider the evidence. Their verdict? — Case Dismissed.

1912 was an eventful year for Johnny. In March he was successfully operated on for appendicitis at the Newport and County Hospital and, on Friday, December 13th, he was again a 'guest' at the Newport Police Court. This time the headline writers had a field day. INTERRUPTED WEDDING screamed the placards. WELL KNOWN BOXER ASSAULTED. ROMANTIC NEWPORT STORY.

Johnny, whose address was given as Ailesbury Street, Newport, was now the complainant and his assailant was no brawny fellow boxer, but Elizabeth Hemming, a smartly dressed young woman from Devon Place. John Moxon again represented Johnny and 'a very romantic story' was told:

Johnny said he had visited the Lyceum Theatre on December 6th with some friends and left there shortly before 10.30p.m. He walked along Bridge Street and had just reached the corner of Cambrian Road when he saw Elizabeth Hemming who suddenly came up to him and struck him a violent blow on the face, causing blood to flow. He kept his hands in his pockets and made no attempt to retaliate.

"I believe all she wants is for you to marry her, and because you will not do so, this is her way of venting her vengeance upon you?" asked Mr Moxon. "Yes," said Johnny.

'Lizzie' Hemming said that Basham was with a young lady. "I went up to him," she said, "because I did not want him to take down the young lady as he has taken down me. When I approached him he said 'Don't you dare to interfere with me,' and I boxed him on the ears."

Did Miss Hemming know that Basham was a professional boxer?

asked the Chairman of the Magistrates. "Yes," she replied "I went with him for fourteen months. The banns were called at St Mark's Church. I had my trousseau, and he had his wedding things, but his mother put a stop to it."

A witness to the assault, Mrs Cornfield, said that Hemming had struck Basham a hard blow in the face and called him bad names. Basham had given no provocation. The blow was a hard one and more than just a box on the ears.

Elizabeth Hemming now returned to the witness box and repeated her allegations. She had kept company with Basham for fourteen months and he had left her in disgrace — "All that is denied," said Mr Moxon, who declined to question Miss Hemming saying, "It is simply a question if the peace is to be maintained."

After hearing from Elizabeth Hemming's mother, the Chairman of the Magistrates, Mr G.R. Martyn summed up. The case would be dismissed, the Bench believing that Elizabeth Hemming had had provocation, but she was warned not to go near or interfere with Basham. Both parties would have to pay their own costs.

But if Johnny thought he was finished with Elizabeth Hemming, he was mistaken. On Friday, September 12th, 1913, when Johnny was still suffering from the traumatic after effects of the Harry Price fight, the Newport Police Court heard Mr Lyndon Cooper mention the case of John Michael Basham, now of Wrexham, who was summoned by Lizzie Hemming to show cause etc. Mr Cooper did not think the case would trouble the Court, as it would probably be arranged, and applied for it to stand over to Monday, an application which was granted. On the Monday, Mr Cooper applied for the case to be withdrawn and the magistrates accepted his application.

Lizzie Hemming apart, nearly everyone seems to have loved Johnny. At his training camp in Wrexham it was not only the soldiers who turned out to watch him and his assortment of flyweights, lightweights and heavyweights go through their paces. As Joe Palmer recalled in 'Recollections of A Boxing Referee,' the youngsters of the town were out in force too:

"So persistent were some of these youngsters that some days there was a string of perambulators outside his training quarters, for nursemaids, whose more mature charges insisted on being brought to watch Basham, could not leave their baby carriages behind."

Even when Johnny's glory days were long gone, the magic still remained. For a time Johnny lived with his brother Sam and his family in

Marion Street, Pill. Sam's son, David John, remembers walking into town with his uncle:

"I was proud to walk with him through the streets of Newport. He had such a following that it took hours to walk from Marion Street to the Market in High Street. Everyone had to speak to Johnny."

Yet, despite all the adulation, Johnny's innate modesty kept shining through. When Sid Worgan met him on Paddington station shortly before the outbreak of World War II, Sid's friend, Jim Daley, asked Johnny what had been his greatest experience? He might have been expected to name the night he took the Lonsdale Belt or any one of his fights but, without hesitation, he chose the Ledoux v. Driscoll fight. He had been mightily impressed by the Frenchman's great sportsmanship when, in the closing rounds, he had refused to press home his advantage against the sick and ailing Welshman.

Johnny Basham began his career as a featherweight and switched to lightweight before becoming a welter. In his early days he stuck rigidly to lemonade and kept well away from alcohol. So well known did he become known eventually that his mere presence was enough to quell what looked like developing into a football "riot" at the F.A. Cup tie between Wrexham and Crewe Alexandra in November, 1919. The crowd had got a little out of control and looked like giving trouble, but a few words from Johnny were enough to quieten them.

Those lucky enough to know Johnny describe him as being like a "feather on his feet in the ring". His hands were "lightning fast" and, in exhibition bouts, the touch of his hand was "as gentle as a sponge on the face". "He was not like a boxer, he was more of a magician". "Johnny would mesmerise you, he was like a magician. Your eyes were fixed on him all the time". The words are those of Edward Donovan, now over one hundred and living in retirement in Newport, who still remembers seeing Johnny line up a row of men and "drop them all with just one touch on the chin".

That Johnny was capable of inspiring deep affection, there is no doubt. The doubts lay in his ability to handle his money properly. Norman Clark said of him:

"Strangely enough, Basham is one of the few good English (sic) boxers who never went to America; but if he had, I am convinced that he would have well held his own with the best in that country". But another Norman, Norman Hurst, had this to say: "Of Basham, a famous American manager who saw him in action said: 'That boy would earn a quarter of a million dollars in America,' then he added, 'and he would no doubt have to work his passage home'".

But if Johnny's financial skills left something to be desired, no one ever doubted his boxing skills or his courage inside the ring. Time after time, he demonstrated his bravery and resourcefulness and, as usual, these qualities were well to the fore when he met his old adversary, lion-hearted Gus Platts, over twenty rounds at the Royal Albert Hall on May 31st, 1921.

At stake were Platts' British and European Middleweight titles, but the match was not recognised officially by either the International Boxing Union, or by the National Sporting Club. The fight began at 8.30 in the evening and Johnny looked in 'fine fettle', having only the previous evening boxed twenty-eight rounds on the lawn at the R.W.F. barracks with partners ranging from flies to heavyweights. This time, too, there had been no trouble making the weight so that, if possible, he was even more cheery than he normally was.

Right from the start Johnny showed plenty of power and speed and scored well with hooks and jabs. He side-stepped, ducked and dodged with characteristic skill and frequently hit Platts half a dozen times without return, but the stolid Yorkshireman resisted heroically, taking all that was thrown at him. He was shaken at times by punches to the jaw, but Johnny's blows lacked their old 'sting' and Platts was able to survive.

The nineteenth round spelled trouble for Johnny as he came out of a clinch, blood pouring profusely from his one eye, so much so that he could hardly see. Sensing his chance, Platts piled on the pressure with the crowd roaring him on, but Johnny was too old and experienced a hand to let slip the titles which now became his. The Platts fight would be Johnny's last win in the professional ring. Never again would he taste the fruits of victory. But if this was to be the last time that Johnny's hand was to be raised in victory by the referee, he still had his Lonsdale Belt and, in the end, only death would take it away from him.

There are still plenty of people living in Newport who can claim to have worn that belt, but it is a privilege denied to their fellow townsmen. The shame of it is that Basham's Belt was ever allowed to leave Newport in the first place. If ever there was a case for municipal intervention, then this, surely, was it. A more far seeing council than the one running Newport at the time would have stepped in to save the Belt and keep it where it rightly belongs — in Wales.

Jim Driscoll's belt is safe and secure in Cardiff and, occasionally, is put on display. For one pound a time people have worn it for charity, a usage which would surely have appealed to Driscoll and to Basham. It may be wishful thinking, but perhaps it is not too late even now for efforts to be made to try and 'rescue' the Belt from its American exile and restore it to its rightful place — with the people of Wales and of Britain. It is just a thought, but maybe its American owner could be persuaded to put it on display in this country.

Mention of Jim Driscoll's belt and its safe haven in Cardiff leads me to compare the contrasting fortunes of the two men after their deaths. Of the two, Driscoll has fared much better. He is 'lionised' and glorified in Cardiff as a hero. Streets are named after him, pub walls bear his photograph, books are written, plays are performed, new hotels name their lounges after the 'Peerless One', there is talk of building a statue.

And Johnny Basham? No Newport street bears his name and, to the best of my knowledge, no photographs of 'The Happy Warrior' adorn the walls of the public houses of his native town. It is true that, at long last, public spirited people have combined to erect a new headstone over his grave but, otherwise, Johnny's name is little celebrated in the town of his birth. It is my hope and fervent wish that this biography will go some way, at least, towards redressing the balance. The last word rests, as it should, with Johnny Basham himself and the anonymous author who entitled his piece, written for a Welsh newspaper in the year 1925, — JOKER JOHNNY BASHAM.

"We were all seated in the Strand Palace Hotel, London, one night when in walked Johnny Basham. He shook hands with each in turn, but left out Driscoll.

"Knowing Basham's affection for Driscoll I did not place any significance on this, though I half-expected some sort of humourous sally. I had not long to wait.

"'Call yourself a man,' began Basham in a well-simulated tone of indignation that checked the buzz of conversation and caused everyone to listen. 'What has he done?' I enquired. 'Done! Nothing at all. Nothing! But that is how he got his Meritorious Medal'.

"Some of those present laughed, others looked inquisitive, while Driscoll himself merely gazed long and hard at Basham with just a faint trace of a provoking smile.

"'Yes,' said Johnny, 'I carried him eight kilometers on my back after he was wounded, and he got rewarded for it. You see, it was just like this: I fell exhausted just as we reached our lines and the Colonel happened to come up. He saw me lying...'

"'How many kilometers did you carry him?' I asked. 'Twelve kilometers,' promptly returned Basham. 'The colonel saw me lying on the

ground and he asked Driscoll what had happened. And what do you think he said? He told the colonel he had carried me in!'

"'But how far did you carry him?' enquired another of the party. 'Fourteen kilometers,' said Basham with emphasis. 'He got the Meritorious Medal and I got put in the guardroom for calling him a hero in Welsh! The whole of my army can tell you the same.' 'Your army?' It was Driscoll who scoffingly put the question. 'Your army?' 'Yes, my army' retorted Basham, 'my army, they were all there'. 'Who do you mean?' I asked. 'Well,' said Johnny, beginning to count on his fingers. 'There was me — Dai Stock — and his dog — and, and — there was myself. We were all there!' Basham kept up his attack in such a bitter and earnest tone that the majority of his hearers were completely deceived until he suddenly held out his hand to Driscoll and said 'How do, Jim, boy!' It was comedy of the best sort."

CHAPTER XVIII

Johnny Basham's Ring Record

Every effort has been made to ensure the accuracy of Johnny's ring record. Some early boxing records, however, are unclear and, sometimes, downright contradictory. Where no day or date is given, this denotes a certain amount of uncertainty attaching to that particular contest.

1908

1. BEAT Hunter — Friday March 6th — Royal Field Artillery Barracks — Newport — Retired in Round Two of Six Round Contest.

2. BEAT Lamprey — Thursday April 9th — Royal Field Artillery Barracks — Newport — Second Round K.O. of Six Round Contest.

3. LOST to Young Murphy — Royal Field Artillery Barracks — Newport — Second Round K.O.

1909

4. BEAT T. Scrivens — Thursday, June 10th — Tredegar Hall — Newport — Six Round Contest — First Round K.O.

5. RESULT UNKNOWN — F. Sydney — Wednesday, July 7th — Tredegar Hall — Newport.

6. BEAT E. Thomas — Friday, July 9th — Tredegar Hall — Newport — Six Two-Minute Round fight.

7. Three Round Exhibition with G. Humphries — Saturday, September 18th — Excelsior Boxing Club — Corporation Road — Newport.

8. BEAT Boxer Ryan — Monday, October 18th — Assault-at-arms — Campbell Bannerman Hall — Wharf Road, Newport — Third Round K.O.

9. Three Round Exhibition with Llew Morgan — Monday, November 22nd — Campbell Bannerman Hall — Newport.

1910

10. LOST to Fred Dyer — Saturday, January 1st — Drill Hall — Newport — Retired Hurt in Fourth Round.

11. LOST to Badger Brian — Monday, January 29th — Badminton Club — Cardiff — Third Round K.O.

12. BEAT Never Jones — Saturday, February 12th — Campbell Bannerman Hall — Newport — Referee Stopped Fight in Tenth Round.

13. BEAT Billy McKeiver — March 2nd — Chepstow — RSF in Third Round.

14. Exhibition with Fred Dyer — March 14th — Cardiff.

15. Three Round Exhibition with W. Lannen — Tuesday, March 29th — Gymnasium — Newport.

16. LOST to Harry Lawrence — April 19th — Chepstow — First Round K.O.

17. Exhibition with G. Hooper — Saturday, May 28th — Lyceum Theatre — Newport.

18. DREW with Phenis Emanuel — June 25th — Newport — Eight Round Contest.

19. Exhibition with Phenis Emanuel — July 9th — Cardiff.

20. BEAT Jimmy Ashen — September 29th — Gloucester — First Round K.O.

21. BEAT Jimmy Ashen — October 8th — Stroud — First Round K.O.

1911

22. DREW with Young Ted Walters — Monday, February 6th — Public Hall — Pontnewydd — Six Round Contest.

23. BEAT Private Taylor — July 29th — Conway Marsh — Fourth Round K.O.

24. BEAT Fred Hayes — Monday, August 7th — Taylor's Pavilion, Rodney Parade — Newport — RSF In Round Eight.

25. BEAT Charlie Price — Thursday, August 10th — Taylor's Pavilion — Newport — In Four Rounds.

26. BEAT Charlie Milestone — August 26th — Wrexham — On Points Over Ten Rounds.

27. BEAT Frank Baker — Saturday, September 23rd — Liverpool — On Points Over Fifteen Rounds.

28. BEAT Charlie Price — Saturday, October 14th — Newport — In Three Rounds.

29. BEAT Charlie Milestone — Wrexham — On Points Over Fifteen Rounds.

30. BEAT Charlie Milestone — October 18th — Wrexham — Thirteenth Round K.O.

31. LOST to Gus Platts — Monday, November 20th — Cardiff — On Points Over Fifteen Rounds.

32. DREW with Nat Williams — Wednesday, November 22nd — Barracks Gymnasium — Wrexham — Over Six Rounds.

33. Exhibition with Harry Treharne — December 18th — Newport.

34. BEAT Tom Mitchell — Thursday, December 28th — Liverpool — Retired In The Eleventh Round.

1912

35. BEAT Harry Berry — Wednesday, February 7th — RWF Depot — Wrexham — On Points Over Fifteen Rounds.

36. Exhibition with Harry Baulch — Thursday, February 8th — Century Institute — Newport.

37. BEAT Harry Berry — Thursday, February 28th — Liverpool — Third Round K.O.

38. Four Round Exhibition with " Battling" Harris — Tuesday, March 5th — Cardiff.

39. BEAT Jack Daniels On Points Over Fifteen Rounds.

40. DREW with Nat Williams Over Fifteen Rounds — Liverpool.

41. BEAT Jack Daniels On Points Over Fifteen Rounds.

42. BEAT Jack Hanley On Points Over Fifteen Rounds.

43. BEAT Badger Brian On Points Over Fifteen Rounds.

44. BEAT Mick Gordon — August 2nd — Liverpool — On Points Over Ten Rounds.

45. BEAT Dick Knock — August 22nd — Liverpool — On Points Over Fifteen Rounds.

46. BEAT Jack Daniels — September 12th — Liverpool — On Points Over Ten Rounds.

47. BEAT Harry Jones — September 18th — Drill Hall — Wrexham — On Points Over Fifteen Rounds.

48. BEAT Jack Langdon — September 26th — Liverpool — Disqualified In Second Round.

49. BEAT Fred Hanley — Wednesday, October 2nd — Chester — On Points Over Ten Rounds.

50. BEAT Dick Knock — Wednesday, October 16th, — Drill Hall — Wrexham — On Points Over Fifteen Rounds.

51. BEAT Jack Daniels — Saturday, October 26th — Drill Hall — Newport — On Points Over Fifteen Rounds.

52. BEAT Ferdinand Quendreux — Thursday, November 7th — Liverpool — On Points Over Fifteen Rounds.

53. BEAT Private Lowe — Tuesday, November 12th — Liverpool — Third Round K.O.

54. BEAT Jack Langdon — Monday, November 18th — Liverpool — Disqualified In Fifteenth Round.

55. BEAT George Colebourne — Thursday, December 5th — Liverpool — On Points Over Fifteen Rounds.

56. BEAT Badger Brian — Saturday, December 14th — Cardiff — On Points Over Twenty Rounds.

57. Four Rounds Exhibition with Charlie Milestone — Monday, December 23rd — Chester.

58. Four Rounds Exhibition with "Young Charlton" — Monday, December 23rd — Chester.

59. LOST to Matt Wells — Thursday, December 26th — Swansea — Seventh Round K.O.

1913

60. BEAT Jack Langdon — Thursday, January 16th — Liverpool — Second Round K.O.

61. Three Round Exhibition with Pritch Proberts — Saturday, January 25th — Swansea.

62. Three Round Exhibition with Badger Brian — Thursday, February 6th — Skating Rink — Chepstow.

63. LOST to Joe Hurst — Thursday, February 20th — Liverpool — On Points After Twenty Rounds.

64. Three Round Exhibition with "Sapper" Jack O' Neill — Tuesday, March 3rd, — Cardiff.

65. LOST to Young Nipper — Wednesday, March 19th — Liverpool — Fifth Round K.O.

66. BEAT Badger Brian — Monday, March 24th — Swansea — On Points Over Fifteen Rounds.

67. DREW with Tom Tees — Thursday, May 22nd — Liverpool — Over Fifteen Rounds.

68. BEAT Harry Jones — Monday, June 16th — Cardiff — Retired End Of Twelfth Round.

69. LOST to Frank Madole — Thursday, June 19th — Liverpool — Retired End Of Second Round.

70. BEAT Frank Madole — Thursday, July 3rd — Liverpool — RSF In Round One.

71. BEAT Frank Madole — Thursday, July 17th — Liverpool — On Points Over Fifteen Rounds.

72. DREW with Tom McCormick — Thursday, July 31st — Liverpool — Over Fifteen Rounds.

73. BEAT Will Brooks — Monday, August 4th — Cardiff — Fourth Round K.O.

74. BEAT Harry Price — Thursday, August 21st — Liverpool — Eleventh Round K.O.

75. BEAT Eddie Beattie — Thursday, October 16th — Liverpool — On Points Over Fifteen Rounds.

76. Three Round Exhibition with Mr. W.J. Kimmer — Saturday, October 25th — Cardiff.

77. BEAT Lance-Sgt. Spalding — Wednesday, October 29th — Barracks Gym — Wrexham — Eighth Round K.O.

78. BEAT Albert Badoud — Thursday, November 20th — Liverpool — On Points Over Fifteen Rounds.

79. BEAT Young Ahearn — Thursday, December 11th — Liverpool — On Points Over Fifteen Rounds.

1914

80. BEAT Albert Badoud — Thursday, January 1st — Liverpool — On Points Over Twenty Rounds.

81. BEAT Young Nipper — Thursday, February 19th — Liverpool — On Points Over Fifteen Rounds.

82. Three Round Exhibition with Jack Webb — Monday, March 9th — Liverpool.

83. BEAT Dick Nelson — Thursday, March 12th — Liverpool — On Points Over Fifteen Rounds.

84. Three Round Exhibition with Willy Hook — Friday, March 27th — Birkenhead.

85. BEAT Henri Demien — Thursday, April 2nd — Liverpool — On Points Over Fifteen Rounds.

86. BEAT Sid Stagg — Monday, April 27th — National Sporting Club — On Points Over Fifteen Rounds.

87. BEAT Gus Platts — Thursday, June 11th — Liverpool — On Points Over Fifteen Rounds.

88. BEAT Johnny Summers — Monday, December 14th — NSC — Ninth Round K.O.

89. Three Round Exhibition with Mr. W. Hazell — Monday, December 21st — NSC.

1915

90. BEAT Johnny Summers — Thursday, February 4th — Liverpool — On Points Over Fifteen Rounds.

91. BEAT Matt Wells — Monday, March 22nd — London Opera House — On Points Over Fifteen Rounds.

92. BEAT Tom McCormick — Monday, May 10th — NSC — Referee Stopped Fight In Thirteenth Round.

93. Three Round Exhibition with Captain H.F.S. Huntington — Saturday, May 22nd — Cardiff.

94. Three Round Exhibition with Griff Griffiths — Saturday, June 19th — Neath.

95. Three Round Exhibition with Jack Conn — Thursday, July 22nd — Liverpool.

96. Three Round Exhibition with Jack Conn — Friday, July 23rd — Liverpool.

97. Three Round Exhibition with Jack Conn — Saturday, July 24th — Sheffield.

98. BEAT Dai Roberts — Thursday, August 12th — Liverpool — Seventh Round K.O.

99. Three Round Exhibition with "Private" Bill Johnson — Saturday, September 4th — Aston.

100. Three Round Exhibition with "Sgt." Walters — Friday, September 24th — Plymouth.

101. Three Round Exhibition with Company Sgt. Maj. Ware — Friday, September 24th — Plymouth.

102. Three Round Exhibition with "Private" Billy Morgan — Saturday, September 25th — Swansea.

103. LOST to Albert Badoud — Thursday, October 21st — Liverpool — Ninth Round K.O.

104. Exhibition with Bat McCarthy — Saturday, December 4th — Empire — Swansea.

1916

105. Three Round Exhibition with Charlie Lucas — Saturday, January 8th — Swansea.

106. Three Round Exhibition with Dai Stock — Saturday, January 8th — Swansea.

Dai Roberts, who fought Johnny in 1915,
and was later killed in action in France.

A detail of Johnny's Lonsdale Belt which he won outright in 1916.

107. BEAT Kid Doyle — Thursday, March 9th — Liverpool — On Points Over Fifteen Rounds.

108. BEAT Eddie Beattie — Monday, May 1st — NSC — RSF in Nineteenth Round.

109. Six Round No Decision Bout with Billy McCarthy — Saturday, May 27th — Tredegar Hall — Newport.

110. BEAT Will Brooks — Saturday, October 7th — Tredegar Hall — Newport — Retired in the Ninth Round.

111. DREW with Gus Platts — Tuesday, December 26th — Liverpool — Over Twenty Rounds.

1917

112. BEAT Will Brooks — Thursday, April 5th — Liverpool — On Points Over Fifteen Rounds.

113. BEAT Sid Burns — Monday, May 28th — Holborn Stadium — London — Retired In Round Nine.

114. BEAT "Private" G.W. Latham — Friday, August 3rd — Aldershot Barracks — On Points Over Six Rounds.

1918

115. BEAT Liscomb Morland — Thursday, February 28th — Liverpool — Retired In Fourteenth Round.

116. BEAT "Sgt" Joe Attwood — Thursday, December 12th — Royal Albert Hall — On Points Over Three Rounds.

117. BEAT "Private" Tierney — Thursday, December 12th — Royal Albert Hall — On Points Over Three Rounds.

118. BEAT Petty Officer Cal Delaney — Thursday, December 12th — Royal Albert Hall — On Points Over Three Rounds. (Inter Services Boxing Association King's Trophy Competition.)

1919

119. BEAT George "Kid" Plested — Saturday, January 4th — Liverpool — Disqualified In Twelfth Round.

120. BEAT Eddie Shevlin — Monday, January 27th — NSC — On Points Over Fifteen Rounds.

121. Four Round Exhibition with Frank Moody — Thursday, January 30th — Tonypandy.

122. BEAT Kid Doyle — Thursday, February 20th — Liverpool — On Points Over Twenty Rounds.

123. BEAT Eddie Shevlin — Monday, March 17th — NSC — On Points Over Twenty Rounds.

124. DREW with Augie Ratner — Monday, June 16th — NSC — Over Twenty Rounds.

125. BEAT Willy Farrell — Monday, July 21st — Liverpool — Retired in Eleventh Round.

126. Three Round Exhibition with Bert Adey — Thursday, July 24th — Pill Athletic Grounds — Newport.

127. BEAT Francis Charles — Thursday, September 2nd — London Olympia — On Points Over Twenty Rounds.

128. BEAT Matt Wells — Thursday, November 13th — Holborn Stadium — London — On Points Over Twenty Rounds.

129. Three Round Exhibition with Geo Griffiths — Friday, November 21st — Drill Hall — Newport.

PROGRAMME.

Under the Direction of CHARLES B. COCHRAN.

REFEREES AND TIMEKEEPERS APPOINTED BY THE EDITOR OF "THE SPORTING LIFE."

6 Three-minute Round Contest.

GEORGE ARCHER (Aldgate) *v.* JIM SKINNER (Chiswick)

Referee: J. T. HULLS, Esq. *Timekeeper:* J. PALMER, Esq.

20 Three-minute Round Contest.

JOHNNY BASHAM (Wrexham) *v.* FRANÇES CHARLES (France)

Welterweight Champion of Great Britain and Holder of Lord Lonsdale Belt

Referee: J. PALMER, Esq. *Timekeeper:* J. T. HULLS, Esq.

20 Three-minute Round Coutest.

JOE BEÇKETT (Southampton) ***v.*** **EDDIE McGOORTY** (Oshkosh, U.S.A.)

Heavyweight Champion of Great Britain

Referee: J. T. HULLS, Esq. *Timekeeper:* J. PALMER, Esq.

10 Three-minute Round Contest.

FRED FULTON (Kansas, U.S.A.) *v.* ARTHUR TOWNLEY (Birkenhead)

Referee: J. PALMER, Esq. *Timekeeper:* J. T. HULLS, Esq.

M.C.: HARRY BREVETT, Esq.

Boxing Gloves used are supplied by John Wisden & Co., Ltd., 23, Cranbourn Street, W.C. 2.

Part of the programme for the Francis Charles v Johnny Basham fight.

130. Exhibition — Saturday, November 22nd — Llwynypia.

1920

131. Three Round Exhibition with "Private" Griffiths — Saturday, February 7th — Swansea.

132. Three Round Exhibition with Frank Moody — Friday, March 5th — Ferndale Working Men's club.

133. BEAT Fred Kay — Monday, April 12th — NSC — On Points Over Twenty Rounds.

134. LOST to Ted Kid Lewis — Wednesday, June 9th — London Olympia — Retired In Round Nine.

135. LOST to Ted Kid Lewis — Friday, November 19th — Royal Albert Hall — Nineteenth Round K.O.

1921

136. Three Round Exhibition with Jack Blackborrow — Saturday, January 29th — Stow Hill Drill Hall — Newport.

137. BEAT Gus Platts — Tuesday, May 24th — Royal Albert Hall — On Points Over Twenty Rounds.

138. LOST to Ted Kid Lewis — Friday, October 14th, — Royal Albert Hall — Retired In Twelfth Round.

1922

139. Three Round Exhibition with Bob Allinson — Saturday, May 13th — Cardiff.

140. Three Round Exhibition with Billy Pritchard — Wednesday, August 30th, Hulme, Manchester.

141. Three Round Exhibition with Albert Johnson — Wednesday, August 30th — Hulme, Manchester.

142. Three Round Exhibition with Jim Scaife — Wednesday — August 30th — Hulme, Manchester.

143. Three Round Exhibition with Ted Llewellyn — Thursday, October 19th — Brecon.

144. Three Round Exhibition with Sgt. Barnes — Thursday, October 19th — Brecon.

The day Johnny stepped into the same ring as Joe Louis.

145. LOST to Mike McTigue — Wednesday — October 25th — Sheffield — Third Round K.O.

1923

//

1924

146. LOST to Jerry Shea — Monday, November 17th — Stow Hill Pavilion — Newport — On Points Over Fifteen Rounds.

147. Three Round Exhibition With Ben Marshall — Wednesday, December 10th — Caldicot Working Men's Club.

1925

148. Three Round Exhibition with Trevor Llewellyn — Monday, April 13th — Cattle Market Stadium — Newport.

149. Three Round Exhibition with Trevor Llewellyn — Saturday, April 18th — Pill Labour Hall — Newport.

150. Three Round Exhibition with Jack Tucker — Saturday, May 30th — Pill Labour Hall — Newport.

1926

151. Three Round Exhibition with Roy Martin — Wednesday, June 23rd — Bargoed New Hall.

152. Three Round Exhibition with Roy Martin — Saturday, June 26th — Bargoed New Hall.

153. Three Round Exhibition with Jeff Bridle — Thursday, July 1st — Pontypool.

154. Two Round Exhibition with Ben Marshall — Thursday, September 9th — British Legion Hall — Pentre.

155. Three Round Exhibition with Ben Marshall — Thursday, September 30th — Mardy.

156. Three Round Exhibition with Jack Newton — Thursday, October 7th — Bedwas.

157. Three Round Exhibition with Fred "Shoeing-smith" Davies — Thursday, November 16th — Caldicot.

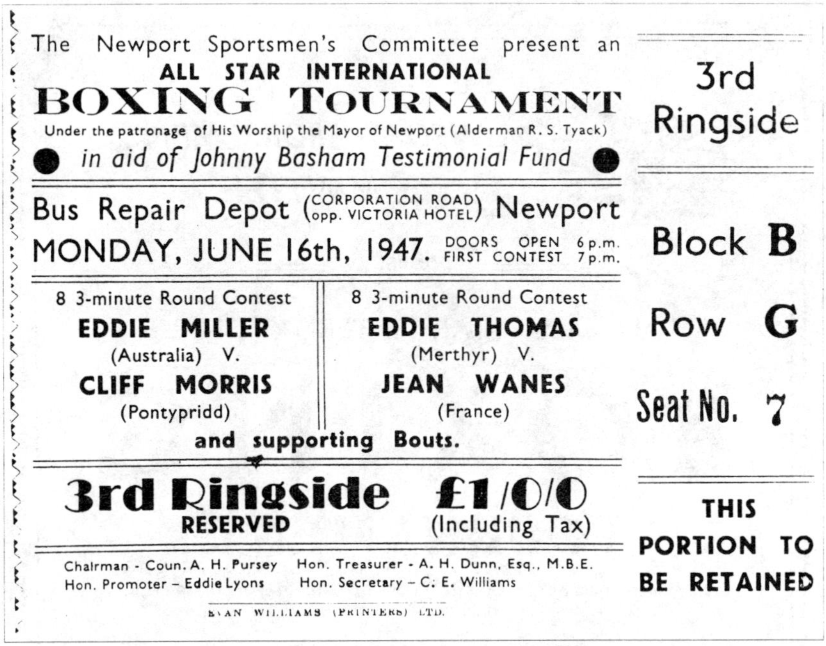

The Newport Sportsmen's Committee present an
ALL STAR INTERNATIONAL
BOXING TOURNAMENT
Under the patronage of His Worship the Mayor of Newport (Alderman R. S. Tyack)
● in aid of Johnny Basham Testimonial Fund ●

Bus Repair Depot (CORPORATION ROAD opp. VICTORIA HOTEL) Newport
MONDAY, JUNE 16th, 1947. DOORS OPEN 6 p.m. FIRST CONTEST 7 p.m.

8 3-minute Round Contest	8 3-minute Round Contest
EDDIE MILLER (Australia) V.	EDDIE THOMAS (Merthyr) V.
CLIFF MORRIS (Pontypridd)	JEAN WANES (France)

and supporting Bouts.

3rd Ringside RESERVED £1/0/0 (Including Tax)

Chairman - Coun. A. H. Pursey
Hon. Treasurer - A. H. Dunn, Esq., M.B.E.
Hon. Promoter - Eddie Lyons
Hon. Secretary - C. E. Williams

EVAN WILLIAMS (PRINTERS) LTD.

3rd Ringside
Block B
Row G
Seat No. 7
THIS PORTION TO BE RETAINED

A reserved ringside ticket for the Johnny Basham Memorial Tournament.

1927

158. Three Round Exhibition with Ben Marshall — Monday, November 7th — Pill Labour Hall — Newport.

159. Three Round Exhibition with Con McCarthy — Saturday, November 12th — Pontypridd.

160. Three Round Exhibition with Lewis Williams — Saturday, November 12th — Pontypridd.

161. Three Round Exhibition with Moss Davies — Saturday, December 3rd — Pandy.

1928

//

NEWPORT SPORTSMEN'S COMMITTEE

present

AN ALL STAR INTERNATIONAL

BOXING

TOURNAMENT

Under the patronage of His Worship the Mayor of Newport
(Alderman R. S. Tyack)

Proceeds in aid of the

"Johnny Basham Memorial Fund"

Newport Corporation
Bus Depot (opp. Hotel Victoria Corporation Road.)
By kind permission of Newport Corporation Transport Committee

Mon., June 16th, 1947.

Official
6d.
Programme

EVAN WILLIAMS (PRINTERS) LTD., NEWPORT.

The front cover of the programme for the Johnny Basham Memorial Tournament.

1929

162. LOST to Ted Kid Lewis — Friday, December 13th — Hoxton Baths — London — RSF in Third Round.

1930-1935

///

1936

163. Six Round Exhibition with Willie Piper — Monday, October 26th — Swansea.

1937

164. Three Round Exhibition with Jack Phillips — "Coronation Day" — May — Shaftesbury Park — Newport.

165. Three Round Exhibition with Arthur Bishop — Saturday, October 22nd — Virginia Park — Caerphilly.

BIBLIOGRAPHY

DENZIL BATCHELOR: Big Fight, The Sportsmans Book Club, London, 1955.

B. BENNISON: Giants On Parade, Rich and Cowan Ltd., 1936.

A.F. BETTINSON AND B. BENNISON: The Home of Boxing, London, Odhams Press Ltd., 1922.

FRANK BUTLER: A History of Boxing in Britain, Arthur Barker Ltd., 1972.

JAMES AND FRANK BUTLER: The Fight Game, The World's Work (1913) Ltd., Kingswood, Surrey, 1954.

JAMES BUTLER: Kings of The Ring, Stanley Paul Ltd., 1936.

HARRY CARPENTER: Masters of Boxing, Heinemann, 1964.

RICARD CHRISTENSEN (DICK NELSON): My Life and My Fights. Twenty Years In The Ring.

NORMAN CLARK: All In The Game, Methuen and Co., 1935.

ALEXANDER CORDELL: Peerless Jim, Hodder and Stoughton, 1984.

"CORINTHIAN": Our Famous Boxers, 1916.

EUGENE CORRI: Thirty Years A Referee, Edward Arnold, 1915.

EUGENE CORRI: Gloves and The Man, Hutchinson and Co., 1927.

EUGENE CORRI: Fifty Years In the Ring, Hutchinson and Co., 1933.

W. BARRINGTON DALBY: Come In Barry. Cassell, London.

FRED DARTNELL: Seconds Out! T. Werner Laurie Ltd., 1924.

GUY DEGHY: Noble and Manly, Hutchinson, 1956.

A.H. DODD: A History Of Wrexham, Hughes and Son, Wrexham, 1957.

HARRY FURNISS: By Ways and Queer Ways of Boxing, 1920.

MAURICE GOLESWORTHY: Encyclopaedia of Boxing, Robert Hale, 1960.

JACK GOODWIN: Myself and My Boxers, Hutchinson, 1924.

JACK GOODWIN AND B.J. EVANS: Boxing, 1922.

ROBERT GRAVES: Goodbye to All That, Jonathan Cape, 1929.

JACK HAILS: Classic Moments of Boxing, Moorland Publishing Co. Ltd., Ashbourne, Derbys., 1983.

G.V. WYNNE JONES: Sports Commentary, Hutchinson's Library of Sports and Pastimes Ltd., 1951.

JAMES KENYON: Boxing History, Methuen and Co. Ltd., 1961.

GILBERT ODD: Great Moments in Sport, Pelham Books, 1974.

GILBERT ODD: Encyclopaedia of Boxing, Hamlyn, 1983.

JOE PALMER: Recollections of a Boxing Referee, Bodley Head, 1927.

CHARLES PLATT: Famous Fights and Fighters, Odhams Press Ltd., 1921.

DOUGLAS SUTHERLAND: The Yellow Earl, Cassell, 1965.

TREVOR C. WIGNALL: The Story of Boxing, Hutchinson and Co., 1923.

TREVOR C. WIGNALL: The Sweet Science, Chapman and Hall, 1926.

TREVOR C. WIGNALL: Prides of the Fancy, Eveleigh Nash and Grayson Ltd., 1928.

INDEX

ACKNOWLEDGEMENTS

For permission to reprint work in copyright I wish to thank the following copyright holders for items from titles listed here:

Century Hutchinson for James Butler's Kings of the Ring; Eugene Corri's Fifty Years in the Ring and Gloves and the Man; Jack Goodwin's Myself and My Boxers; G.V. Wynne Jones's Sports Commentary.

Chapman and Hall Ltd. for Trevor C. Wignall's The Sweet Science.

Hodder and Stoughton Ltd. for Alexander Cordell's Peerless Jim.

Nyt Nordisk Forlag-Arnold Busck A/S for Dick Nelson's Mit fur og mine Kampe (My Life and My Fights).

A.P. Watt Ltd. on behalf of the Executors of the Estate of Robert Graves for Robert Graves's Goodbye To All That.

I was greatly helped in my research by the Bodleian Library, Oxford; the British Library-Newspaper Library; Christie's the London auctioneers; Durham County Library; Liverpool City Library, the National Library of Wales, Aberystwyth; Newport Reference Library; South Glamorgan County Library, Cardiff and Wrexham Library.

My special thanks go to those members of the Basham family who took the time and trouble to talk to me about Johnny: the late Mrs. Winifred Shutt, his sister, Mrs. Lilian Watson, his sister-in-law. Mrs. M. Pero and Mrs. K. Tayler, his nieces and Mr. D.J.E. Basham and Mr. Vincent Williams, his nephews.

I would also like to thank the following Newportonians who helped me in their differing ways: Patrick White of the Newport Local History Society for his help with written material. Louise Reeves for research into Johnny's family background. John Briggs, Allen Lloyd and Jim Sullivan for their photographic work. Les Coulson, Edward Donovan, Stella Ingram, Bob Madden, Jim Ryan, Mr. and Mrs. Sellwood, George Setterland, Les Thomas for sharing their memories of Johnny with me. Bill Dennison, Richard Frame, John Francis, Graham Greenway, Sister Irene, Phil Muirden, Dick Murray, Ty Richardson and Sam Basham for their invaluable help and advice.

From Swansea I received help from Desmond Burns, Cliff Curvis, John Lannen, Cliff Mahoney, Arthur Rayne Williams and John Wishart. Glyn Moses and Catherine Flynn (Cardiff) were very helpful as were Ron Dibbin (Blaina), Eddie Thomas (Merthyr), Sid Worgan (Llantrisant) and Boxing Historian Arthur R. Watkins of Cwm, Ebbw Vale who alerted me to the existence of two of Johnny's earliest fights.

From Wrexham and North Wales I received help from Mrs. L. Down, R.J. Evans, Bobby Fielding, E. Jennings, Mr. Pais, Mrs. Roberts, The Royal Welch Fusiliers, "Silin" of the "Wrexham Leader" and Evelyn Walker.

Thanks also to the following from the other side of "Offa's Dyke": Fred Deakin for keeping me supplied with old records of Johnny's past exploits. Dan Richardt of Denmark for letting me know about Dick Nelson's book and providing me with the basis of a translation. Harold Alderman, boxing historian, for a detailed copy of Johnny's ring record. John Morris, the Secretary of the British Boxing Board of Control. Gilbert Odd, boxing historian. Dave Collette, W.J. Collette, Reg Gutteridge, Barry Hugman, Bill Jones, Reuben Jones, Michael D. Lerwill, Ken Moiser and Brigadier (R) M.H. ap Rhys Pryce, all of whom were kind enough to respond to my appeals for information.

For picture permissions I would like to thank Patrick White of Newport for allowing me to photograph and reproduce many of the illustrations in the book. Cliff V. Knight for an early photograph of Johnny from Pillgwenlly: Newport, published by Starling Press, Risca, 1983. Gerald Steen of Wrexham and the Clwyd County Record Office for the picture of Johnny arriving at the Duke of Wellington by charabanc. The National Library of Wales for reproducing three photographs. The South Wales Argus for the photos of stone masons working on Johnny's headstone and the inauguration ceremony at the graveside. The Hulton Picture Company (Hulton Deutsch) for the picture of Johnny and Kid Lewis at the weigh-in for their second fight. Syndication International for the photograph of Johnny and the "Kid" locked in combat. The Evening Standard for Tom Webster's cartoons. Pelham Books for permission to reproduce the photograph of Johnny and the Kid from Great Moments in Sport, copyright Gilbert Odd 1973. South Glamorgan County Library for the photograph of the six First World War Army Boxing Instructors. Mrs. Down of Wrexham for the photograph of Johnny and his two soldier comrades. Bozena Roderick for her photographs of the wooden cross marking Johnny Basham's grave and also of the author on the back cover of JOHNNY!

Thanks also to the following who gave me valuable pre-publication publicity: Bill Barrett of the Cardiff Herald and Free Post, Mike Buckingham of the South Wales Argus, Syd Dye of the Liverpool Echo, "Silin" of the Wrexham Leader, The Editor of the Boxing News, Charlotte Evans of BBC Radio Gwent, Don John, Editor of the Newport and Cwmbran Herald and Free Post, Peter Johnson of BBC Radio Wales,

The Newport Free Press, Guy Stock of Marcher Sound, Wrexham, "Westgate" of the Western Mail, and all those others who helped to publicise my venture in their own way — my grateful thanks to you all.

I would also like to thank Edward Arnold (Publishers) for permission to quote from '30 Years a Referee' by Eugene Corri.

I could not finish without thanking my typesetters, Dave and Rachel of Uppercase in Cardiff, Stuart Hill of Design Plus, Cwmbran who designed the cover of JOHNNY! and everyone at Starling Press, Risca.

If, after all that, I have left anyone out — let me assure you that any such omissions were purely unintentional and I renew my thanks to all of you here.

LIST OF SUBSCRIBERS

I wish to thank each and every one of my subscribers. Without their aid and assistance, JOHNNY! might never have seen the light of day. So, once again, I offer my thanks to:

LES "KID BASHAM" ADAMS, 13 Rhosrhedyn, Southsea, Wrexham, Clwyd.

JACK AGLAND, Isca Steel Stock, Unit 28, Star Trading Estate, Caerleon, Gwent.

JIM AHERN, Newport, Gwent.

GILBERT ALLNUTT, Hon. Secretary, Croydon Ex-Boxers' Association, 25 Melrose Avenue, Norbury, London.

ASSOCIATED BRITISH PORTS, Alexandra Dock, Newport, Gwent.

AUBREY & IRENE, The Lyceum Tavern, Malpas Road, Newport, Gwent.

ALAN BAILEY, The White Hart Inn, Llangibby, near Usk, Gwent.

JIM BAINBOROUGH, London Ex-Boxers' Association, 276 Dunlin .House, Gurnell Grove, Ealing, London.

BARCLAYS BANK PLC, 14 Commercial Street, Newport, Gwent.

HARRY BARNBROOK, The Station Restaurant, Bassaleg, Newport, Gwent.

BILL BARRETT, 7 Bronwydd Close, Penylan, Cardiff, South Glamorgan.

DAVE BARTON, West of England Pub, Mill Parade, Newport, Gwent.

D.J.E. BASHAM, 36 Churchill Road, Walton, Stone, Staffordshire.

IAN BASHAM, The Coronation Club, Newport, Gwent.

MIKE BASHAM, Newport, Gwent.

SAM BASHAM, Newport, Gwent.

STEVE BASHAM, Newport, Gwent.

BASS & WELSH BREWERS TAVERNS, Maes-y-Coed Road, Cardiff, South Glamorgan.

ALAN BEATTIE, The Oaks, Itton, Chepstow, Gwent.

NEIL M. BELLERS, 71 Marvels Lane, London.

BIG G'S PIZZA RESTAURANT, 370 Chepstow Road, Newport, Gwent.

ABNER BLACKSTOCK, Phoenix Boxing Club, Newport, Gwent.

STEVE BLANKS, The Talisman, Commercial Road, Newport, Gwent.

WINSTON BODDY, The Waterloo Hotel, Alexandra Road, Newport, Gwent.

BOOKWORM, Skinner Street, Newport, Gwent.

ROGER & DIANE BOSWELL, Engineers Arms, Newport, Gwent.

BOWATER SPORTS AND SOCIAL CLUB, Alexandra Dock, Newport, Gwent.

BOXING MONTHLY, 24 Notting Hill Gate, London.

PETER BRANCH, 247 Goodwin Close, Warminster, Wiltshire.

Mr. LARRY BRAYSHER, 22 Belmont Road, Bushey, Hertfordshire.

BRIAN & MARY, Hereford Arms, Maindee, Newport, Gwent.

PAUL BRITCH, Secretary, St. Helens Ex-Boxers' Association, Exchange Vaults, Cooper Street, St. Helens.

JOE BUTTIGIEG, Parc Close, Llangibby, Gwent.

MIKE BUCKINGHAM, South Wales Argus, Maesglas, Newport, Gwent.

CALDICOT COMPREHENSIVE ART DEPARTMENT, Caldicot Comprehensive, Caldicot, Gwent.

CALDICOT COMPREHENSIVE SCHOOL, Caldicot, Gwent.

J. CARPENTER, Handpost Hotel, Ansells, Newport, Gwent.

HARRY CARROL, Royal Oak Boxing Club, Cardiff, South Glamorgan.

IAN & LORRAINE CASHMAN, The Welsh Oak, Rogerstone, Newport, Gwent.

CASNEWYDD RESTAURANT, 54 Cardiff Road, Newport, Gwent.

CAXTON TAXIS, 16 Baneswell Road, Newport, Gwent.

MARTIN CHAPMAN, c/o United News Shops, The Handpost, Newport, Gwent.

CHELTENHAM AND GLOUCESTER BUILDING SOCIETY, Newport, Gwent.

G. CODD, Newport, Gwent.

COLIN & CAROLYN CHILVER, 74 Longford Street, Middlesborough, Cleveland.

E.A. COLE, Church House Inn, Portland Street, Newport, Gwent.

ALEXANDER CORDELL, Rhosddu, Wrexham, Clwyd.

HENRY CORDY & SON LIMITED, 2/3 Station Approach, Newport, Gwent.

CRINDAU HARLEQUIN AMATEUR BOXING CLUB, Newport, Gwent.

JIM CROWLEY, Avon Close, Bettws, Newport, Gwent.

MARTIN CULLIFORD, Newport, Gwent.

THEO DAVIES, Swansea, West Glamorgan.

PAUL DIAPER, Eurotours, Newport, Gwent.

PETER DISSON, Kriegsstrasse 56, Oberhausen, West Germany.
DOCKS CONSERVATIVE CLUB, 1 Pottery Terrace, Newport, Gwent.
MICHAEL A. DOHERTY, Newport, Gwent.
Mr. & Mrs. PETER DRAVE, Newport, Gwent.
JIM DYER, Newport, Gwent.
IKE EDWARDS, The Jolly Roger, Rogerstone, Newport, Gwent.
PHIL EDWARDS, Ex-Middleweight Champion of Wales, Cardiff, South Glamorgan.
Mr. ELIAS, NHSOB Club, Stow Hill, Newport, Gwent.
JEAN ELLIS, Handpost Stores, Stow Hill, Newport, Gwent.
N.T. ELLIS, Linnard and Ellis, Chartered Accountants, 2 Risca Road, Newport, Gwent.
DAVID N. FORD, 11 Lowlands Road, Pontnewydd, Cwmbran, Gwent.
W.J. FOULSER, 8 St. Georges Crescent, Abergavenny, Gwent.
A.J. FOUWEATHER, Heating and Plumbing, 127 Caerleon Road, Newport, Gwent.
ALFRED FOWLER (Ex-Boxer), 44 Heol-y-Pentre, Pentyrch, Cardiff, South Glamorgan.
RICHARD FRAME, Newport, Gwent.
JULIAN FRENCH, The Gladiator, Pillmawr Road, Newport, Gwent.
V. GABICA & SONS, Scrap Merchants, Walsall Street, Newport, Gwent.
L.G. GIBBONS, 3 Carlton Road, Newport, Gwent.
PHILLIP GIULIETTI, Newport, Gwent.
THE GUNNER CLUB, 24 Pottery Terrace, Newport, Gwent.
A.W. HARDY, London Ex-Boxers' Association, 148 Marcus Avenue, Thorpe Bay, Essex.
R.A. HARTLEY, 542 Kings Drive, Wembley, Middlesex.
BRETT HAYES, Maindee, Newport, Gwent.
Mrs. HAYWARD, 37 Wilmot Green, Warley, Brentwood, Essex.
Mr. S.N. HEMMING, 203 Heritage Park, St. Mellons, Cardiff.
ALAN HENSHALL, 2 St. Edward Street, Newport, Gwent.
J.M. HIGHLEY, The Greyhound, High Street, Newport, Gwent.
STUART HILL, Design Plus, Powys House, South Walk, Cwmbran, Gwent.
Mr. LEE-HING, The Alma, Commercial Road, Pill, Newport, Gwent.
M. HOLLAND, Newport, Gwent.
PAUL HOPE, Editor/Publisher "Spitbucket", 20 Muffett Close, Victoria Drive, Wimbledon, London.

C. HOWELLS, 11 Danylan, Llanelli, Dyfed.
HUGMAN SPORTING PUBLICATIONS LIMITED, 24 Notting Hill Gate, London.
THE IRISH CLUB, Commercial Road, Pill, Newport, Gwent.
GUNTER JAKOB, Johann-Peter-Hebel-Realschule, Waghausel, West Germany.
MORRIS JAMES, 3 Ceulan Terrace, Talybont, Aberystwyth, Dyfed.
JANET & GORDON, The Myrtle Grove, Pontymister, Risca, Gwent.
DAVID JENKINS, Glasllwch Lane, Newport, Gwent.
KEN JENNER, The Cedars, Llanbadoc, Usk, Gwent.
JEWEL OF INDIA, Tandoori Restaurant, 368 Chepstow Road, Newport, Gwent.
IAN & JACKIE JOHNSON, The Six Bells, Stow Hill, Newport, Gwent.
ALLAN E. JONES, 31 The Avenue, Caldicot, Gwent.
BILL JONES, 3 Gordon Drive, Grassendale, Liverpool.
DAVID JONES, Caldicot Comprehensive School, Caldicot, Gwent.
Mr. & Mrs. D. JONES, The Risca House Inn, Commercial Street, Risca, Gwent.
GEORGE JONES, Newport, Gwent.
KEVIN JONES, The Flat, Gobowen W.M. Club, Old Whittington Road, Gobowen, Near Oswestry, Salop.
REUBEN JONES, 28 Mornington Crescent, Mackworth, Derby.
RICHARD THOMAS JONES, The Man of Gwent, Chepstow Road, Newport, Gwent.
ROBERT JONES, Gate Hangs High, Rhosnesni, Wrexham, Clwyd.
RON JONES, Chairman of Gwent County Council.
SAM JONES, S.A. JONES & SONS CARPETS, Newport, Gwent.
ALAN KERSHAW, Llangibby, Gwent.
KOH-I-NOOR TANDOORI RESTAURANT, 164 Chepstow Road, Maindee, Newport, Gwent.
LAUREL CONSTRUCTION AND MARINE, Newport, Gwent.
BRIAN LAWRENSON, Baileys Real Ale, Newport, Gwent.
LEICESTER & DISTRICT EX-BOXERS' ASSOCIATION, 60 Dumbleton Avenue, Leicester.
BRIAN LEWIS, Cotton Club, Newport, Gwent.
DAVID JOHN LEWIS, 29 Tredegar Terrace, Cross Keys, Gwent.
T.A. LEWIS, Carpenters Arms, Hall of Fame, Newport, Gwent.
T. LEWIS, Parc-y-Prior, Malpas, Newport, Gwent.
Mr. & Mrs. G. LOUKA, The Princess Restaurant, 50 Cambrian Road, Newport, Gwent.

JOHN LOVELOCK, Ivy Bush Inn, Clarence Place, Newport, Gwent.
JOHN & BARBARA LUXFORD, Oddfellows Arms, 137 Duckpool Road, Maindee, Newport, Gwent.
PETER McINNES, P.F. & J.R. McInnes, 59 Richmond Park Road, Bournemouth, Dorset.
EDWARD McLOUGHLIN, Newport, Gwent.
Mr. R.H. MAIN, The Goldcroft Inn, Caerleon, Gwent.
EDDIE MAIS, Newport, Gwent.
DENNIS P. MALONEY, 40 Coverack Road, Newport, Gwent.
MARCUS MUSIC, Tredegar House, Newport, Gwent.
R. MARSHALL, Newport, Gwent.
MARIE MARSTON, Alexandra Inn, Commercial Road, Pill, Newport, Gwent.
ANTHONY PAUL MARTIN, 60 Hollybush Road, Cyn-Coed, Cardiff, South Glamorgan.
MERVYN MASON, 40 Bourne Avenue, Kirkby-In-Ashfield, Nottinghamshire.
MARK MASSOW, 67 Woodcote Avenue, Elm Park, Hornchurch, Essex.
JOHN MATTHEWS, 39 Cypress Grove, Hainault, Ilford, Essex.
SARAG MEAH, Helal Tandoori Indian Restaurant, 168 Chepstow Road, Newport, Gwent.
ALAN & CILLA MICHAEL, Royal Albert, Maindee, Newport, Gwent.
MIDLAND BANK, Bridge Street, Newport, Gwent.
KEN MOISER, Newbolt Road, Balby, Doncaster, South Yorkshire.
W.S. MOORE, Monumental Sculptors, 160 Malpas Road, Newport, Gwent.
ANDREW RICHARD MORGAN, 72 Risca Road, Newport, Gwent.
HOWARD & JULIE MORGAN, The Windsor Castle, 19 Upper Dock Street, Newport, Gwent.
VERNON & JO MORGAN, Manor Hotel, 147 Stow Hill, Newport, Gwent.
DENIS MORRISON, Hon. Secretary, Irish Ex-Boxers' Association, 55 Philipsburgh Terrace, Marino, Dublin, Ireland.
GLYN MOSES, Cardiff, South Glamorgan.
A.M. NARDUZZO LIMITED, 39/43 Malpas Road, Newport, Gwent.
NATIONWIDE BUILDING SOCIETY, Newport, Gwent.
NEWPORT LOCAL HISTORY SOCIETY, Newport, Gwent.
JOHN O' KEEFE, The Priory Hotel, Caerleon, Gwent.

DAVID OSMOND, 3 Woodville Road, Newport, Gwent.
MARK PEARCE, Lloyds Public House, Newport, Gwent.
Mrs. MARILYN PERO, Caldicot Street, Newport, Gwent.
PILL LABOUR CLUB, James Street, Newport, Gwent.
STUART & REBECCA PINNELL, 64 Manor Street, Heath, Cardiff, South Glamorgan.
BRIAN POWELL, 138 Laurel Road, Bassaleg, Newport, Gwent.
JACK POWELL, Secretary, London Ex-Boxers' Association, 36 St. Peter's Street, London.
JONATHAN PREECE, Llanfrechfa, Cwmbran, Gwent.
Mr. GRAHAM A. QUICK, Miskin, Pontyclun, Mid Glamorgan.
RGM SUPPLIES, 81 Alexandra Road, Newport, Gwent.
PAUL RAWLINGS, Caldicot Comprehensive School, Gwent.
BILL REED, Green Lane, Caldicot, Gwent.
M. REYNOLDS, Cross Hands, Chepstow Road, Newport, Gwent.
JOHN RICHARDS, Diverse Music, 185 Upper Dock Street, Newport, Gwent.
TY RICHARDSON, The Angel and The Lamb, Newport, Gwent.
RIVER VIEW CLUB, Newport, Gwent.
Mr. & Mrs. ROACH, New Griffin Hotel, Brynmawr, Gwent.
KEN ROBINSON, 181 Ash-Lea Drive, Donnington, Telford, Shropshire.
B.R. RODERICK, 45 Lockwood Crescent, Whyalla, South Australia.
C.A. RODERICK, The Gaer, Newport, Gwent.
R.T. RODERICK, 31 Beechwood Crescent, Newport, Gwent.
S.A. RODERICK, London.
T. RODERICK, The Gaer, Newport, Gwent.
Mr. & Mrs. ALBERT ROWLANDS, 39 Marysfield Close, Marshfield, Cardiff.
ALBERT RYAN, Llanthewy Road, Newport, Gwent.
J.L. RYAN, Newport, Gwent.
St. MARY'S PARISH, Newport, Gwent.
RALPH & MARLENE SHALOM, The Robin Hood Inn, Bufflers Holt, Brackley Road, Buckingham, Buckinghamshire.
JOHN SHINE, Shine Food Machinery Ltd., 260A-262 Corporation Road, Newport, Gwent.
W.E. SHORT, 3 Clist Walk, Bettws, Newport, Gwent.
WALTER SIMPSON, Baneswell, Newport, Gwent.
STEVE SIMS, (Ex-British Featherweight Champion), The Welsh Prince, Commercial Street, Newport, Gwent.

NIGEL E. SKENDROVIC, 80 Blackwatch Road, Radford, Coventry.
DAI SMITH, University of Wales, Cardiff, South Glamorgan.
DAVID SMITH, Anderley Lodge, 216 Stow Hill, Newport, Gwent.
WALTER SPENCER, 37 Clifford Avenue, Beeston, Nottingham.
G.D. STEPHENS, M.B.E., 117 Bulwer Road, London.
STILLS DESIGN GROUP, Lower Dock Street, Newport, Gwent.
JOHN STONEMAN, 79 Fields Park Road, Newport, Gwent.
PETER STRONG, Caldicot Comprehensive School, Caldicot, Gwent.
P.O. SULLIVAN, Newport, Gwent.
Mrs. K. TAYLER, 35 Dart Road, Bettws Estate, Newport, Gwent.
R. TAYLER & SON, Building Services, Unit 3, Jacks Pill Industrial Estate, East Dock Road, Newport, Gwent.
TAYLORS D-I-Y, 12 Malpas Road, Newport, Gwent.
Mr. F.G. TAYLOR, Secretary, Plymouth Ex-Boxers' Association, 11 Exmouth Road, Devonport, Plymouth, Devon.
W.C. TAYLOR, 54 Cardiff Road, Newport, Gwent.
GILBERT THOMAS, 6 Jarman Avenue, Huntroyde, Wrexham, Clwyd.
RUSSELL T. THOMAS, Butchers, Newport Market, Newport, Gwent.
MAURICE THORRINGTON, Canton Indoor Market, 1A Leckwith Road, Canton, Cardiff, South Glamorgan.
Mr. THOMAS TOWNSON, 15 Caryl Grove, Liverpool.
TIMM & NIKE, Heidelberg, West Germany.
Mr. IAN TRICK, Kerricabs Limited, Newport, Gwent.
TROUTMARK, Books and Records, Newport Market, Newport, Gwent.
L.R. TURNBULL, General Engineering Services Ltd., Collingdon Road, Cardiff, South Glamorgan.
A.D. TURNER & SONS, Family Butchers, Newport Market, Newport, Gwent.
CLIFFORD VERNON, Son of G.H. Vernon, Moss. 49 Coed Efa, New Broughton, Wrexham, Clwyd.
BOB VICKERY, Managing Director, Epco Electronics Limited, Unit 3, Taverner Industrial Estate, Caerleon, Newport, Gwent.
WALLIS AND BLACKBOROW ROOFING, Newport, Gwent.
Mr. R. WALLIS, Chimneys Guest House, Pentonville, Newport, Gwent.
Mr. & Mrs. WALSH, The Olway Inn, Old Chepstow Road, Llangeview, Near Usk, Gwent.
N.C. WARD, 235 Burton Road, Lincoln.
WASHERCRAFT, Charles Street, Newport, Gwent.

COLIN WATERS, Newport Sporting Club, Newport, Gwent.

ARTHUR R. WATKINS, Boxing Historian, 32 Curre Street, Cwm, Ebbw Vale, Gwent.

Mrs. LILIAN WATSON, Caldicot, Gwent.

WELCH OF NEWPORT, Atlas Garage, Turner Street, Newport, Gwent.

MARTIN & ZOE WHATMORE, Crown Inn, Crown Street, Maindee, Newport, Gwent.

HARRY WHEELER, Fruit Merchants, Market Street, Newport, Gwent.

Mrs. FRANCES WHEELHOUSE, Dyers, 42 Stoneham Street, Coggeshall, Essex.

DOUG WILLIAMS, Chepstow, Gwent.

GERALD WILLIAMS, Newport, Gwent.

MAC WILLIAMS, Royal Oak Boxing Club, Cardiff, South Glamorgan.

PAUL WILLIAMS, Newport, Gwent.

PETER & RAE WILLIAMS, Kings Arms, Pill, Newport, Gwent.

Mr. V. WILLIAMS (Proprietor The Carpet Shop, Pontypridd), 25 Pontfaen Road, Newport, Gwent.

WILLIAMS BROS (NPT) Ltd., 121, Lower Dock Street, Newport, Gwent.

JOHN WILSON, Newport, Gwent.

MALCOLM GILLIES WILSON, 10 Raphael Close, Newport, Gwent.

GEORGE WITHERINGTON, 188 Camberwell Grove, London.

BILL WOLLEN, Newport, Gwent.

TONY & PAT WOODWARD, 47 Stoke Road, Linslade, Leighton Buzzard, Bedfordshire.

DORIAN WOOLLEY, Glanwern Grove, Newport, Gwent.

Mrs. WREN, 17 Tewithall Close, Speke, Liverpool.

WYE VALLEY VINTNERS, St. Woolos Wine Lodge, Stow Hill, Newport, Gwent.

JOHN & CATHERINE WYSOME, 61 Allt-yr-yn Road, Newport, Gwent.

ABOUT THE AUTHOR

Alan Roderick was born in Newport, Gwent on September 23rd, 1946. He was educated at St. Mary's Primary School, Duffryn High School and later Bradford University, where he graduated with a Joint Honours Degree in French and German in 1969. In 1975 he completed a one year Teacher Training course at the University College of North Wales, Bangor.

Since leaving university he has worked with the BBC Monitoring Service in Reading and taught in Nottingham and London, before spending five years teaching English as a Foreign Language to secondary school students in West Germany.

After returning to Wales he decided to put his knowledge of foreign languages to good use and, since May 1979, he has been employed by Gwent County Council as a teacher of French and German at Caldicot Comprehensive School. He is married and lives in Newport.

In 1980 he won the Local History Competition organised by the Gwent Local History Society and the South Wales Argus with a History of the Welsh Language in Gwent. Other books followed — JOHNNY! THE STORY OF THE HAPPY WARRIOR is his seventh — and there have also been a number of articles published in a variety of newspapers and magazines.

ORDER FORM

Heron Press
84 Llanthewy Road
NEWPORT, Gwent, NP9 4LA
Telephone: (0633) 250 302

Please send me the following books by Alan Roderick:

.........copies of JOHNNY! THE STORY OF THE HAPPY WARRIOR @ £7.95 each. (Postage and Packing £1 extra)

.........copies of THE MUSIC OF FAIR TONGUES — THE STORY OF THE WELSH LANGUAGE IN GWENT @ £1.50 each. (Postage and Packing 25p extra)

PRE-PAYMENT WITH ORDER, PLEASE.

I enclose a cheque or postal order made out to Heron Press:

NAME..

....

ADDRESS...

....

....

....

.... POST CODE ....